Best Kept Secrets
Michigan Back Roads

Have Fun

by *Ron*

Ron Rademacher

First Edition

Back Roads Publications
Nahma, Michigan

Best Kept Secrets – Michigan Back Roads

PAGE NUMBERS MAP

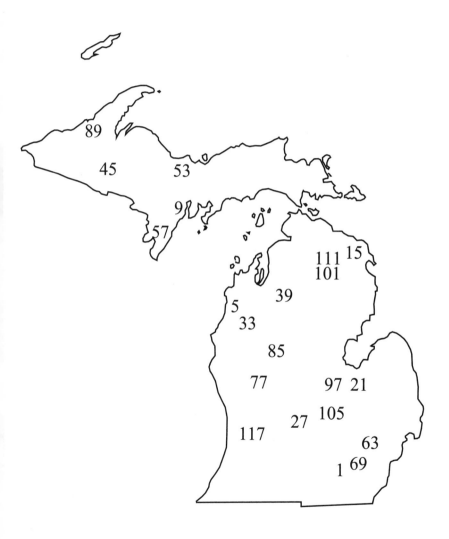

TABLE OF CONTENTS

Best Kept Secrets Michigan Back Roads

by

Ron Rademacher

Back Roads Publication
P. O. Box 458.
Rapid River, Michigan 49878

Unless stated otherwise, all content is the opinion of the author, and does not constitute legal or travel advice.

The author accepts no responsibility for the content or accuracy of information on third party websites.

Acknowledgments

This one wouldn't have been written without the support of the chapter sponsors.

Cover Photograph - The Ledges – "Adventure Awaits" Cover photograph by Christian Keathleyad

Thanks are due to all the people in the small Michigan towns who have made time for my presentations, endless questions and photographic intrusions.

A special thanks to the Grand Ledge Chamber of Commerce and Grand Ledge DDA for sponsoring this project.

Best Kept Secrets
Michigan Back Roads

by Ron Rademacher

Published by
Back Roads Publications
Nahma, Michigan

ISBN 978-0-9883138-7-3

ANAGAMA

When you see the Anagama for the first time you may be completely underwhelmed. From the outside it is unremarkable, just a long narrow shed with a curved roof. In fact, the 4,000 square foot ceramics gallery, a few steps away, seems way more impressive. First impressions can be misleading. The long and the short of it is, the Albion Anagama is the largest single-chamber wood-fired kiln in the United States. The term anagama is a Japanese term meaning "cave kiln". When you see the cave kiln blasting away, it is plenty impressive. Ken Shenstone is the artist behind the kiln and the gallery. He, and David Habicht, built the anagama along with the other three kilns on the property. Some of the bricks used in the 55 foot by 14 foot kiln came from the old Malleable Forge building in Albion.

The anagama is big, with an interior capacity of about 1,000 cubic feet. The kiln is heated by wood and is capable of producing ceramic objects on an impressive scale. There are other types of kilns that are easier to use. The anagama consumes a lot of wood. When the kiln is running at its hottest, it can burn as much as a face cord per half hour. That is a stack of firewood that would be 4 feet high and 8 feet long. With all this capacity, one might wonder what in the world one would use it for. Why would you need a kiln that is more than 50 feet in length. After the kiln was constructed 1987, Mr. Shenstone fired it up for a demonstration, and started an

October tradition that continues today.

Every autumn potters and clay sculptors gather in Albion for the firing. The artists bring objects they have been preparing all year. A massive quantity of wood has been gathered and the anagama has been readied. For the next 10 days the kiln will run without interruption. More than 2,000 pieces of pottery will be fired during the 240 hour cycle. The kiln requires attention 24 hours per day during the 10 day event. Artists, crafters and volunteers handle the work. The wood has been donated by Albion resident Rusty Hull, who receives artwork in return. Some artists will bring meals. Others will split wood or tend the fire. Their reward is a small space in the kiln where their clay creations will be transformed into gorgeous pottery. Night and day the work, some say party, goes on without a break. At the end, works of art are the reward for all the work. Plain earthenware clay is put in. Beautiful inspired works of pottery come out.

The firing of the Anagama is one of many Albion events in October. If you decide to stay, the innkeepers know all the local secrets. There are two bed and breakfasts in town the Albion Heritage B&B and the Palmer House B&B. Both are historic buildings that have been beautifully preserved. The innkeepers at both are excellent cooks and they know all details about history and what is going on around town. The Palmer House was built in the 1800s and has a 19th Century atmosphere with 21st Century amenities. The atmosphere is created by the period antiques throughout the home. The rooms each feature unique antiques. The Albion Heritage Bed and Breakfast occupies a stately Georgian Revival home, built in 1912. With the finest of amenities; Queen-sized beds, private baths, shower massage jets, towel warmers, cable TV/DVD/VHS/CD, wireless Internet connection, air conditioning, and gourmet breakfasts.

THE

ARCADIA

MARCH

BOARDWALK

OPENED

TO

THE

PUBLIC

FOR

BIRDWATCHING

IN

2019

ARCADIA MARSH BOARDWALK

Birdwatching has become the number one outdoor activity in Michigan. In summer of 2019 a bird habitat that has previously been difficult at best will become easily accessible to birders for the first time. In fact, the Arcadia Marsh Preserve is expected to be one of the top 10 birdwatching destinations in Michigan. The Arcadia Marsh Preserve Boardwalk will provide visitors with unparalleled access to a rare ecosystem; a Great Lakes Coastal Marsh. Great Lakes marshes are unique areas where the land and water meet. It has been estimated that 80% of the original Great Lakes Marshes have been lost. Marsh ecosystems are very productive, and the Arcadia Marsh is one of only about 15 that remain on Lake Michigan in the lower peninsula. Once, there was only a short trail on the edge of the marsh. Now a broad ¾ mile long boardwalk will extend from the parking area, across the inland water, into the heart of the marsh itself. The boardwalk follows an old railroad grade. It is suspended two feet above ground-level due to lake levels variations and to protect native plants and soil. The plans include a path for hiking, bump-outs with benches, observation platforms and accessible fishing piers. This state-of-the-art boardwalk will make the nature area accessible to everyone, regardless of mobility issues. Interpretive signs will be placed at regular intervals explaining what makes a marsh important to water quality as well as describing the views. To protect the wildlife that depends on the marsh, the boardwalk will be closed at certain nesting times.

The Arcadia Marsh is rare for size as well, more than 270 acres of wetland have been protected in the Preserve. At last count, it was determined that more than 180 species of birds can be found there. Watchers gather to observe the migrating waterfowl like blue and green herons along with sand hill cranes. Endangered and threatened species can be found here as well, seventeen at last tally. Birders can add several species to their logs. This is an easy place to find American and Least Bitterns. Rare birds that have been spotted in the interior of the marsh include Bewick's Wren, the Black-billed Magpie, Purple Gallinule and Nelson's Sparrow; none of which I could identify. The boardwalk will be a boon in the winter months when rough-legged hawks and snowy owls have been reported. In all seasons the marsh is home to deer, mink, otters and marsh hare, not to mention 25+ species of fish. Another unique feature of the Arcadia Marsh is the wild rice. The Conservancy is partnering with area tribes to restore the wild rice beds that once flourished here. "River" rice, known as "manoomin", was native to the Manistee area and was an important traditional food source. The marsh with its shallow waters and slow currents is ideal for the cultivation of River rice.

A BIT OF HISTORY

The marsh, about 400 acres, fed by Bowen's Creek, has absorbed a lot of punishment over the years. If you think of time geologically, it has been one doggone thing after another. In the1800s, a railroad was constructed through the marsh. In the 1950s, the water level was drained to improve local agriculture, people like to eat you know. Bowens Creek was diverted twice during all this and has become rather shallow, slow and filled with sediment. Later, M-22 was built across Arcadia Lake. That causeway is only about a quarter mile long, but only one narrow channel was created to preserve a connection between Acadia Lake to the Arcadia Marsh. In 2010, the Grand Traverse Regional Land Conservancy acquired 155 acres within the marsh. They teamed up with some local groups and got to work fixing things. They got water flowing through the original channel of Bowens Creek. A controlled burn was staged to remove some invasive species. Six acres of open water were created to attract migrating birds and aid northern pike on their spawning run. Finally, the boardwalk was added.

Pure water played a central part at another historic destination nearby. Pierport was an important village during the lumber era. Some histories claim that Pierport was the first town in Michigan where every home had indoor running water. This was a time when indoor plumbing was nearly unknown in the small villages and towns on the frontier. The secret for Pierport was the high water table and great water pressure. They claimed that if you shoved a pipe into the ground you would tap right into an artesian well, and the water would begin to flow. You can find evidence of these artesian wells right at the intersection of the road to Pierport and the Natural Beauty Road that runs along Lake Michigan. There on the side of the road is pipe sticking out of the ground spouting pure cold water. The plaque beside the water says "Old Faceful". The other feature that makes this a fun stop is the beach. Just a few feet from the "Old Faceful" is Lake Michigan. There you will find a small sandy beach that is perfect of a picnic.

There is much more to discover around Arcadia. Luckily there is first rate lodging right in the village. The innkeepers at the Arcadia House Bed & Breakfast, Carriage House & Mini Spa know the area intimately. They sharing all the best that Northwestern Michigan has to offer while you enjoy gracious accommodations, outstanding breakfasts and peaceful starry nights. The Arcadia House is located at 17304 Northwood Hwy (Scenic M-22) Arcadia, Michigan 49613

ESCANABA

Someone once said that there is no such thing as bad publicity. I'm not so sure. Escanaba In Da Moonlight holds the record for the longest running play in Detroit's history. The film was a success but didn't do any favors for Escanaba. That film has given most people who have never been to Escanaba, a distorted view of what life is like there. Escanaba isn't a primitive wilderness and the weather isn't always like that seen in the movie.

Approaching Escanaba from any direction is going to put the visitor at the junction of Route 2 and Route 41. These roads are on the edge of town where the fast food places and many services are located. To get into downtown Escanaba to explore the really cool stuff, head south at that junction where the huge banner over the entire street welcomes you to downtown Escanaba. This is where the unique character of this upper peninsula town begins to become apparent. The road to downtown is a broad boulevard with five lanes. Shops, local dining spots and brew pubs line the street. The sidewalks are broad as well, making it easy to enjoy the many festivals and events that take place there. To get a true idea of life in Escanaba, one needs to know about the beaches, the arts and the banana belt.

Of course, when talking about beautiful beaches, Escanaba may not spring to mind, but Escanaba has beaches and they are gorgeous. Little Bay de Noc, part of

Lake Michigan, is where you find the Escanaba Municipal Beach. It is part of Ludington Park. The beach is found on a small island connected to the main park by a road and a footpath. In addition to the warm sand and clear clean water, the beach has a bath house with changing rooms, showers and bathrooms. There is an area set aside for picnics with an adjacent playground. Just a short distance away is a boat launch and a fishing pier that is handicap accessible. During the summer season there are lifeguards on duty. When beachgoers have had enough sun, the Sand Point Lighthouse and Delta County Historical Museum are within walking distance. To get to the park and beach just drive all the way through downtown on that broad boulevard to the marina.

Another beach is found inside the Portage Point State Wildlife Area south of town. This beach is on a strip of land that extends out into Lake Michigan for nearly two miles, Portage Point. As would be expected the beach is more isolated but has the added advantage of some great nature features. There are places to launch a canoe or kayak. There is also a walking path on a raised dike that allows visitors to hike through the marsh and wetlands to see the wildlife and do a little birdwatching especially during the spring and fall migrations. There are no facilities at the beach, take what you need, but the beach has lots of room and dogs on leashes are welcome.

Whether driving to a beach, another nature area or downtown for a little shopping, visitors quickly notice the public works all through town. The sculptures are evidence of the vibrant arts community. Some of the pieces reflect the popularity of sport fishing in the region, others depict local history, some the maritime influence of the Great Lakes. One group of sculptures is unique to the upper peninsula. That group is the several pieces that make up "Walk of the Planets". The walk is comprised of 12 stations and illustrates the distances between the planets of the Solar System. The walk and sculptures are in the north side of Ludington St. The walk begins at the Escanaba Public Library and runs to the Anderson Funeral Home, near Lincoln Road. That last station is the Space Probe, Voyager I, launched in 1978.

More superb art can be found in the downtown galleries. The East Ludington Gallery is the oldest artist cooperative gallery in the Upper Peninsula. The gallery has become a favorite destination for lovers of art of all kinds. There are more than 40 artists contributing to the works at the gallery from functional crafts to fine arts. Inside are found paintings in several mediums, stained glass, jewelry, photography and quilts among many others. The gallery has high standards for what will be displayed. All artists must have their work juried before the gallery will accept it. The gallery is inside an historic building and consists of several rooms. Whether searching for a simple craft item of a complex piece of fine art, it can be found here, and the quality is always of the highest.

Just a short walk from the East Ludington Gallery is the William Bonifas Fine Arts Center. It is considered home to all the arts in the Central Upper Peninsula. There are galleries to tour, art workshops, educational classes and theatrical productions. The galleries feature local and regional art exhibits. Their programs and classes are designed to offer educational opportunities for all ages and all skill levels. Whether a beginner or an accomplished artist, the Bonifas is a resource that can offer new insights. The Alice Powers Gallery offers traveling exhibits by regional artists that change throughout the year. Items displayed cover several media like pottery, sculpture and paintings. Some works of art can be purchased at the Kasota gift shop inside the center. According to their mission statement, "William Bonifas Fine Arts Center is a comprehensive arts organization. With a commitment to excellence in its exhibits, education, performances, facilities, events and other activities. The Center exists to enhance and inspire the cultural and creative lives of the people in the Central Upper Peninsula." There is no charge to visit the galleries.

Besides the prevalence of the arts, another thing that surprises people is the pleasant weather. Sure, they have winter weather, this is the upper peninsula, but it is more clement than many expect. There is a section of the upper peninsula known as the Banana Belt. It runs through the center of the peninsula from west to east and has much milder weather due to lake effect winds and other factors. Escanaba is within the western part of the belt and gets less snow than Lansing and much less than Traverse City. On one trip I was in Felch, about 45 minutes away, where we got 12 inches of snow one night. When I arrived in Escanaba next morning, they had gotten less than an inch. The weather is pleasant enough of the time to support a superb farmers market. At the pavilion are found local produce and a variety of items created by local artists and crafters.

The weather is one of the things that convinced the upper peninsula folks to have a fair. It started in 1928 and was held every year. Then in 2010 funding for the Upper Peninsula State Fair and the Michigan State Fair near Detroit was ended. When that happened the 15 counties of the upper peninsula, plus the Hannahville Indian Community, pulled together with resources and volunteers to make Escanaba home to Michigan's only State Fair. This fair is the real deal. For a full week in August, the third week, it is fun for everyone. They have an old fashion midway, shows at the grandstand entertainment and all of the fair type foods one could hope for. In recent years attendance has exceeded 80,000 fun seekers. There is something for the whole family; from horses to lambs, antique cars and race cars, and fireworks on Sunday, it is a sensational State Fair. I don't think any of this was in the movie.

VISITORS

ARE

ALLOWED

TO

TAKE

25 POUNDS

OF

FOSSILS

FROM

ROCKPORT

FOSSIL QUARRY & VIRGIN PINES

A full day of adventure with virgin pines, a quarry full of fossils, sinkholes and an abandoned village can be found at the Rockport State Park Recreation Area. Like most State Parks there is a picnic area, a fishing pier, and sanitation facilities. Aside from those amenities, most everything about this destination is different. There is a pier once used to load limestone on to Great Lakes ore ships. The old limestone quarry is vast. There are sinkholes, bat caves, virgin pines, an abandoned village and some of the most rugged trails anywhere in Michigan.

Upon entering the recreation area there are a couple of options. To the right is a parking area and boat launch providing access to Lake Huron. This is also where the vault toilets are located. To the left is another parking area adjacent to the picnic area and the old pier which is now a popular fishing spot. It is from this area that the trailhead to the various sections of the park is found. There may be interpretive signs at hand, depending on the season. Another benefit of the remote character of this area is the near total lack of light after sundown. That means very dark skies and brilliant stars. From time to time the Aurora Borealis can be seen. Take what you need with you, there are no shops at the park, and you have 4,000 acres of wild Michigan to explore.

Rock hounds think they are in fossil heaven when they discover the old quarry. It covers 300 acres and is crisscrossed by trails. The quarry is only a few yards from the parking area, but once you are in just a little bit you are struck by the view. The landscape looks like a planet from some science fiction movie. The ground is rugged with wave after wave of detritus from the days when limestone was mined here. In the distance is a sinkhole area and cliffs that beckon the adventurous. Everywhere you look fossils are scattered all over the ground. The trail through the quarry is rough and rugged, really, really, rough. The ground is uneven and covered with loose rocks. Those rocks have sharp edges, so this is no place for flip flops. I wouldn't go in without stout shoes or hiking boots. There is no shade in the quarry, so in the summer months those rocks reflect a lot of heat. When searching for fossils it can be handy to keep a couple things in mind. First, warm rocks in the sun are a favorite hangout for snakes. Most species here are harmless but expect to find a few sunbathing on any given day. Second, if you decide to leave the trail to check out a distant boulder or two, pause to get oriented first. The landscape has few distinguishing features, so it is easy to lose sight of where the trail anytime you leave it. After you are done checking out that boulder and look around, everything looks the same in every direction. It isn't that you won't be able to find your way out. It is just that, as rough as the trail is, the land off the trail is rougher and much more difficult to move through compared to being on the trail. The rock covered ground makes keeping your balance a little sketchy at times. If you never understood the phrase "hard scrabble" before, you will after just a short time in this place. The fossils and the surreal scenery make it all worth it. Visitors may to take fossils home, up to 25 pounds per person.

There are sinkholes throughout the park. There are trails beyond the quarry that lead to the sinkhole area, a dozen sinkholes can be located by the determined hiker. Most of them are dry, but one of them is now lake, more than 100 feet deep, and full of fish. The water is coming up from an underground aquifer. These sinkholes are part of the karst geology of this entire region and were formed by water erosion causing the limestone below to collapse. The plant life at the bottom of these sinkholes can be completely different from that which is found in the surrounding area. The environment at the bottom is different due to temperature variations and the way the light gets down there. While it is possible to get right up to the edge of several of the sinkholes, entering or climbing down into them is not recommended. Again, the trails out to the sinkhole area are quite rough, still some people do ride mountain bikes on them.

From the parking area, walking north along the shoreline a trail will lead to old conveyor tunnels used during the mining operations. Those tunnels are now occupied by three species of bats. Making a home there are big brown bats, little brown bats and tri-colored bats. The tunnel entrances are blocked by grates designed to keep intruders out while allowing the bats to come and go. They are active in the warm months and hibernate inside the tunnels in the winter. Interpretive signs are nearby explaining the different species of bats and their importance to the environment.

At the northern most end of the Recreation Area is another entrance that leads to a stand of Virgin White Pines. This is designated as the Besser Natural Area. The Besser Natural Area is quite compact and there is a decent sign that illustrates the trail system which is one simple loop. There are a couple of small side trails but sticking to the main trail makes for a nice short hike. I chose to go left from the sign which will take the visitor into the forest. About half-way around the loop is a stone monument describing the stand of virgin pines that surround it. Continuing on a short distance there is another side trail that leads to the abandoned village of Bell. Don't expect a cool ghost town or anything like that. There are a few foundations and a restored chimney with fireplace. Further along, the main trail curves to follow the shoreline of Lake Huron back toward the parking area. There are side trails to the water and a few clearings. In one of those clearings is a rather large abandoned safe with the door blown off. No idea of the age or origin of the safe.

DIRECTIONS – The Rockport Recreation Area is about 10 miles south of Rogers City off Route 23. Look for Rockport Dr. The last couple of miles to the parking area

are gravel. The Besser Natural Area is north on Route 23.
Take Rayburn Highway east to the Recreation Area sign.
The road to the Besser parking area is gravel. A
Recreation Pass is required. Drive time from Grayling is
2.5 about hours.

FRANKENMUTH

MICHIGAN

IS

KNOWN

AS

LITTLE

BAVARIA

FRANKENMUTH

Frankenmuth, Michigan is far more famous than most subjects found in the Michigan Back Roads books. Almost everybody has heard about Zehnders for chicken dinners, Bonners Christmas Store and the world-famous Bavarian Inn. Frankenmuth is famous for those places, as well as my favorite, the World Expo of Beer. However, there are a couple of destinations in Frankenmuth that can be missed with all the crowds and excitement. Something is almost always happening in town, after all, they have 18 festivals each year. The three attractions that got me all wound up are a restaurant, a cruise, and a unique manufacturing operation dealing with wool off the hoof.

The Old Christmas Station Restaurant is important to locate because a day trip to Frankenmuth is a day full of action and a dining break is going to be necessary. It is right at the main intersection up the hill. In a town with a plethora of dining spots, the Old Christmas Station Restaurant is still a standout. They prepare authentic European dishes from scratch, so you can count on delicious and top-notch quality. I can't tell you about everything on the menu, because I keep going back for the same two dishes. They offer the best Schnitzel I have had outside Germany and seem to be the only people around who know how to make Austrian Goulash. I struggle between schnitzel and goulash, every time I visit.

For those less fortunate who haven't had it, schnitzel refers to thin cuts of meat, breaded and fried. Wienerschnitzel is Austrian Schnitzel made with veal. The German recipe, known as Schweineschnitzel, uses pork. Regardless of the one you choose at the Old Christmas Station Restaurant you will plan to come back for more. When I want to avoid fried and breaded, the Austrian goulash is my automatic choice. Hungarian goulash is common in Michigan and may be soupy and usually contains bell peppers. Austrian goulash only contains beef and onions. The tender beef is coated in a thick, dark, and smooth gravy, made without any thickening agents like flour or sour cream. All Christmas Station recipes are prepared from scratch, so plan on a little wait time, this place will be packed during season. The portions are big so you may have to get the Black Forest Cake to go.

Frankenmuth is inland from any of the Great Lakes or any lake for that matter, so that cool cruise is on a river. This isn't just a ride on the water, this is a cruise that is built around two treats, wine and chocolate. The cruise "ships" are electric ducky boats called funships. The Frankenmuth FunShips can be found between the Frankenmuth Brewery and the Herzog Hotel at the top of the hill. The cruise boats operate on the river behind the hill, away from the chaos and frenzy downtown. You just climb aboard, kick back and enjoy the cruise while indulging in a wine and chocolate tasting.

There is so much to see and do on a getaway to Frankenmuth that many visitors miss the best kept secret of all, the woolen mill. The Frankenmuth Woolen Mill has been in continuous operation since 1894 making it the oldest woolen mill in Michigan. When you enter you are in a clean, modern showroom and retail shop. On display are samples of the products that are manufactured on site, pillows, comforters, mattress toppers and dryer balls. In addition, they offer custom wool processing, organic wool bedding, wool roving and wool batting. The real prize inside is the tour of the historic wool processing facility.

The mill uses only California wool using carbon beneficial farming methods from just three farms. An adult sheep can produce about 15 pounds of wool per shearing. A bale of wool weighs in at around 300 pounds and they process around 500 bales each year. They process all this raw wool by hand or using cog and belt driven machinery, much of which was installed in the early 1900s. There are no computer driven machines in use. Through a wall to wall window at the back of the retail space is a view of part of the mill. There is a line of bathtubs where the wool is washed by hand before being put into the giant spinner that removes the moister. That spinner has been in use since 1903. When the moister has been extracted, the wool is moved to a drying room where it will require 3-5 days to air dry. The wool is then ready to be pulled/picked by hand.

Several processing steps are done by hand, the others use vintage machines with names like mule, carding machine, doffer, picker and fly shuttle loom. Each machine plays a part and the tour demonstrates or explains what each machine does. When planning to take the tour remember that some of the processing areas are warm. The use of steam and humidity control eliminate the need to use chemicals. High humidity in the work rooms also prevents the development of static electricity. As the tour continues the old bookkeeping system is revealed. What it consists of are hand-written notes penciled onto the walls and beams. The notes may mention the weight of a shipment or a problem that needs to be solved. Some of the inscriptions are 100 years old.

All this careful work and attention to detail results in the best quality wool for use in organic wool bedding with well-known benefits. The wool is soft and will not cause itching. Wool is non-flammable so no fire-retardant chemical treatment is necessary, as would be with cotton. Dust mites don't live in wool, it dries too fast. Wool bedding is great for sufferers of fibromyalgia and arthritis because wool is supportive and distributes weight evenly. Allergy sufferers swear by the mattress toppers and comforters. The mill also does custom processing for people who raise sheep. Each batch receives the same careful handling before the wool is used in a custom-made comforter.

The tour of the woolen mill is great fun for children. Young people who have never seen a belt driven machine the size of a Chevy van, are fascinated and are always taking selfies. Scattered throughout the facility are wonderful old photographs from days gone by, don't overlook them. It is a good idea to call ahead or check online for tour schedules.

There is another good reason to plan a trip to Frankenmuth, festivals. There are at least 18 festivals and events every year. That works out to a shindig every three weeks. A big one is in the Christmas season when people come from all over the world to tour Bronner's and add to their tree ornament collection. My favorites are earlier in the year. The World Expo of Beer taps the keg on the third weekend in May every year. The Expo is the largest beer sampling event in Michigan. Years past have seen almost 400 different beers from around the world. Another festival that draws thousands is the Frankenmuth Dog Bowl. This isn't one of those inside an arena where dogs trot around a track. This is an Olympic-style festival with all manner of events and competitions, the largest in the world. The dogs love it. The herding breeds get to herd, the water dogs get to leap into great pools of water, the weiner dogs race with visions of left over schnitzel dancing in their heads. To top it off, there is the hot air balloon event, Balloons over Bavarian Inn. The whole shebang is free and family friendly.

GRAND

LEDGE

WAS

FAMOUS

AS

THE

LOCATION

OF

THE

SEVEN

ISLANDS

RESORT

GRAND LEDGE

When we think of wilderness pathways, islands in the river and soaring cliffs we usually think of northern Michigan or, perhaps, the upper peninsula. On the other hand, there is a place in southern known to Native Americans as "Big Rocks" that has all of these features and a few others as well. The tribe led by Chief Okemos made their way to "Big Rocks" each spring to tap the maple trees for sap to make syrup. Settler histories tell of the caves that were scattered through the area known as the Robbers Caves by some and Counterfeiters Caves by others. Tales were told of stolen horses being hidden in the caves. Other stories claimed that runaway slaves were hidden there as they made their way to Canada along the underground railroad. The "Big Rocks" area is now known as Grand Ledge. Along the Grand River are picturesque sandstone ledges and seven islands in the river. The ledges have been a local favorite for nearly a century. As high as 60 feet above the river, the combination of the great rock cliffs and the explosion of colorful leaves in autumn on the surrounding hardwoods, make this a color tour that is perhaps the best in southern Michigan.

There are several ways to get in close and enjoy these unique formations. One of the easiest ways to get to the ledges is through popular Fitzgerald Park. There are trails for hiking and cross-country skiing, disc golf and other sports fields, picnic areas and the barn theatre. Just follow the paved pathway past the Red Barn Theatre and you will come to steps leading down to the Grand River. The walking trail follows the river and provides great access to the ledges. There are interpretive signs along the way to explain the geology and history. Visible in the river are the seven islands, where the Seven Island Resort once operated, and the railroad trestle. Another way to the ledges is via Oak Park on W. Front Street giving access to the ledges on the opposite side of the river. Finally, the ledges and the river can be enjoyed by paddling up from Jaycee Park or on a cruise on the paddle boat, River Princess.

As fascinating as the ledges are, there is another nature area that may be the only one of its kind in lower Michigan. North of town on Tallman Road is where Lincoln Brick Park is found. When driving into the park on a gravel road, everything appears to be normal. There are tall beautiful trees, a prairie reclamation project, as one would expect, and then, there are those unexpected ruins. They don't look like much, just a couple of walls and a chimney, but they are the first clue to what was once here. Moving further into the park, observant visitors may notice enormous mounds. Those mounds are actually piles of fallen brick. In addition to the mounds are an old quarry, half buried derelict machinery and more ruins. The park is comprised of 90 acres of recreation area and thousands of feet of river frontage. Nice trails meander through the ruins with interpretive signs at key points of interest, the trails also wind through the woods, past the playgrounds and on around the old quarry.

The ruins and mounds of bricks are all that remain of the Grand Ledge Brick Company. The kiln was 300 feet long and was in production for over 100 years. There were 11 buildings in the complex stretching from the quarry to the kilns, connected by railroad tracks. The factory manufactured hundreds of thousands of bricks that were used in buildings that are still standing. A local legend claims that when the quarry and the old brick kilns shut down, a giant steam shovel was abandoned in the quarry and is now underwater. That quarry is a swimming spot favored by the locals.

There are many more parks and nature areas in the Grand Ledge area. Another that is worth knowing about is the Jaycee Park located directly behind the Opera House. The park is on the banks of the Grand River, has a fine kayak and boat launch. Using the park is one of the best ways to paddle to the seven islands and the ledges. Jaycee Park is also the venue for several festivals and musical events throughout the year. All Eaton County parks are dog friendly, but leashes are mandatory.

With all the natural beauty to enjoy time flies by and it's be easy to miss a stroll through downtown. There are shops, dining spots, history and art. One distinctive building is the historic Opera House. The Opera House began as a roller rink in 1884 when Grand Ledge was a major destination. It then became an opera house, a venue for theatrical shows and local events. In its long life it has served as a movie theatre, a furniture store and warehouse. The Opera House continues to serve the community as an event venue to this day. Across the street is a gallery dedicated to local artists and crafters. Just a block from the Opera House is the foot bridge across the Grand River to Island Park where the Island Art Fair has been held for decades. Festivals and events are an important part of life in Grand Ledge. Downtown is also where fun seekers gather for the Annual Victorian Days Festival, the St. Patrick's Day Parade famous for the Irish Stew cook off and the Christmas Parade. One event that continues to grow in popularity is the Color Cruise on the Grand River held the second week in October every fall. The festival includes crafters, vintage exhibits and great food. The star of the show is the is the stern wheel paddleboat. Passengers cruise the river to photograph the famous ledges and marvel at the fall colors.

If you decide to stay in town after dark, you might plan to visit the Fox Park Observatory. Fox Park is another that is maintained by Eaton County Parks as part of their memorable outdoor experiences. The observatory has a Potterville address but is only a couple miles away. They offer regular programs throughout the year. The equipment that is available to the public is top quality including automated controls. That means amateurs can see some real celestial wonders like the rings of Saturn, distant galaxies and at times a passing comet.

With so much to see and do, a map or guide brochure would come in handy. Both are available from the Grand Ledge Chamber of Commerce office or from their website.

KALEVA

HAS

THE

ONLY

REMAINING

INTACT

STRUCTURE

CONSTRUCTED

WITH

BOTTLES

IN

MICHIGAN

KALEVA

Many people hear about the Village of Kaleva because of a house built with bottles. There really is a Bottle House. Not only that, there are other unusual attractions scattered around the village. Kaleva is easy to miss, in spite of the fact that it is on a scenic road "up north" only a few miles east of Lake Michigan. Many people drive right by because the road doesn't go through the center of town. It does pass right by the excellent Kaleva Roadside Park, however. In a village full of surprises, the park could be the best kept secret of all. This isn't one of those little roadside parks you see along the highways with a couple of picnic tables and a dog run. This is a campground with all the amenities.

The park is large enough to have a lighted softball field, a gazebo, playground and a lot of mature maple trees to provide shade. The park contains several campsites, both modern and primitive. There is also a dump station, and rates are very reasonable. The park is a perfect spot from which to explore the history, art, shops and restaurants in Kaleva. Despite of the fact that the park is so affordable, full of amenities and convenient, there is usually a spot or two open. There are exceptions to this. The park is usually full to capacity during the popular Kaleva Days Festival and it can fill up on weekends in the fall when the salmon season is in full swing. Some people come to this area just for the fishing. The High Bridge boat launch on the Manistee River is just a short drive away.

Best known of the local attractions is the Bottle House. One of the most unique buildings in Michigan, the Bottle House was built after a random discovery. John Makinen operated a bottling plant in Kaleva. The discovery had to do with insulation. He noticed that soda pop in bottles stored in his warehouse didn't freeze during the cold northern Michigan winters. It was by this observation that he discovered the insulating properties of his bottles and, he had an idea. There just might be a use for the thousands of flawed and chipped bottles that were set aside during quality control inspections.

Mr. Makinen was an inventive man. He created a special cementing mixture that could be used to bind the bottles together into walls. With that process, he set about using more than 60,000 of his bottles to build his home which became known as the Bottle House. Being artistic as well as industrious, Mr. Makinen wove different colored bottles into designs and words into the walls of the house including "Happy" on one side of the front door and "Home" on the other side. The bottle house was a popular success and neighbors had him build a few other structures around town, but they have all been torn down. The Bottle House is still there and houses the Historical Museum. While touring the inside, the bottles are not visible, since the walls are finished like any other home of the period. The insulating properties of the bottles come in handy on a hot summer day, the ten inch thick walls keep the indoor temperature a good 10 degrees cooler than outdoors.

Another Makinen, William this time, was also a manufacturing artist. He created the Makinen Tackle Company to produce fishing lures. By 1946 the company had expanded to fifty employees from the Kaleva area. In 1945 Makinen Tackle sold 135,000 lures. A room in the Bottle House Museum is dedicated to company he created.

While touring the museum, be sure to go into the small room at the back of the house. On the walls of that room are six beautiful and extremely rare murals. The murals were created during the Great Depression under the auspices of the Work Projects Administration. The WPA sponsored projects, large and small, all over Michigan, to put people to work. A well-known artist of the time, Harry Armstrong, was directed to help communities develop an art project that would reflect local history or culture. The project chosen for Kaleva was these murals depicting an epic poem, the Kalevela. The poem tells the Finnish creation story. Mr. Armstrong sketched the images onto the panels and local children painted the scenes in brilliant colors that still burst forth. Written records of the Kalevela, in English, are difficult to find. These gorgeous murals, show the creation of the world, populated by dwarfs, princesses, gods, goblins, and a host of other mythical creatures. The Kalevela Murals survived the passing of time hung on the walls of the high school gymnasium. After many years they were taken in by the Historical Society and moved to the Bottle House Museum. The murals alone are worth the trip.

Kaleva is compact enough that you could see the whole town on a walking tour. The Centennial Walkway is a pleasant pathway and introduces visitors to the healthy arts community that thrives here. The walkway follows the old railroad grade at the west end of town. All along the walkway are sculptures and works of art related to the history of Kaleva. One sculpture always gets the most attention. You can't miss the giant grasshopper; it's 18 feet long and weighs in at 500 pounds. As so often happens here, there is a Finnish connection. The story goes that St. Urho chased all the grasshoppers out of Finland. It had to be done because, year after year, they kept eating the entire grape crop. St. Urho did miss one grasshopper. It got away and came to Kaleva. The event is commemorated on March 16th, St. Urho's day.

With works of art at every turn, it is no surprise that there is an art gallery in town. The gallery building was the headquarters for an area newspaper, the Siirtolainen, meaning Immigrant. Then it became the village drug store for many years. Now it is an art cooperative featuring the works of local artists. Preserving their traditions and history has always been important to the residents, even the street names are taken from the Kalevela. Another preservation example is the small log cabin theatre near the library. This structure, an old fashion style Finnish log cabin, was home to a family with 6 members. Now it is the venue for free concerts on Friday evenings every August. Between the Centennial Walkway and the Log Cabin is the Railroad Depot Museum. It preserves the history of the impact the lumbering industry and the railroad had on this entire region.

KALKASKA

HOSTS

THE

NATIONAL

TROUT

FESTIVAL

AND

THE

ICEMAN

COMETH

BICYCLE

RACE

KALKASKA

Northwest Michigan has become one of the top regions for vacationers and rightfully so. The area has everything. There are famous sand dunes, rivers for kayakers and fishermen, festivals, huge forests and miles of trails. People who make their way to the northwest for the first time are sometimes surprised to discover that they can't get there on the Interstate Highway System. At some point on the trip they will have to travel on a Michigan back road and, unless your route hugs the shore of Lake Michigan, the journey will very likely pass through Kalkaska. Even the North Country Trail and the Iron Belle hiking trails go through Kalkaska County. Embraced by the Pere Marquette State Forest and within a few miles of major shopping destinations, Kalkaska has developed as a sort of headquarters for sports lovers and nature lovers. It's almost like everyone who goes there just loves to play outdoors. Throw in some major festival events and you have a town that really is a favorite destination in all four seasons.

Kalkaska is a designated Trail Town courtesy of the North Country Trail Association. Several miles of the NCT and the Iron Belle Trail pass through the Pere Marquette Forest and into town. The Iron Belle shares a portion of the North Country Trail. More walking trails are found in the Skegemog Natural Area, the School Forest, and others. A favorite, and seldom visited trail, winds through the Seven Bridges Park, known as the "Jewel of Kalkaska County". Seven Bridges is west of town on the road to Rapid River. There is only a small parking area off the side of the road and a small sign that announces the park. As you walk in you will begin to hear the sound of tumbling water and just a few feet down the rustic path you will spot the first bridge. By the time you pass the first bridge of the seven bridges you will have left the everyday world behind and entered a world of tranquil natural beauty. The trail wanders through a shady forest, the banks of the streams covered in wildflowers. The trail is only a mile long, the bridges are connected by boardwalks where the going is damp. Rapid River and its tributaries are blue ribbon trout streams so it isn't unusual to spot anglers working a favorite spot. There are trails for sports other than hiking. Kayakers can explore the Boardman River and Rapid River. ORV enthusiasts gather at the The Leetsville ORV Trailhead. The system offers more than 20 miles of off road trail riding. Bicycle trails abound as well and not just in the warm months. Kalkaska is home to a major winter event for the bicycle, The Iceman Cometh Race.

The Iceman Cometh is an event that illustrates the genius Kalkaskans have for combining the local natural beauty with a festival. This event takes place every November. November usually means cold and snow in this part of Michigan. That doesn't stop the iceman racers, in fact, the weather is part of the fun. They set off to cover nearly thirty miles of paved roads, dirt roads, snake trails, two tracks and abandoned railroad trails. The race begins at the Kalkaska Airport and treats spectators to racers traversing the gravel and the grasslands. Then they plunge into the forest to make their way past landmarks like "Steve's Secret", "Lombard's Luge" and the "Icebreaker". The race finishes near Traverse City after covering the famous VASA Nordic Ski Trail. The event is a race and a party, and they have been at it for 30 years.

Downtown Kalkaska is the venue for several events; three of them remain on my "must do" list every year. Kalkaska is on a major railroad route and the railroad is still in use here. In June they have a most unusual event, the Speeder Cars come to town. Speeder Cars are railroad motor cars that were used by safety inspectors and to move maintenance crews quickly. They were mainly boxy affairs that could move faster than walkers or those using a hand car. Each year dozens of speeder cars make the excursion from Petoskey to Cadillac with a stop at Chalker Park in downtown Kalkaska. Some of them have been tricked out for the event. There is even one speeder that has the body of a mini Cooper, one of only five in the world. The Speeder Cars stop in town for a while so spectators can get pictures and check out these very cool vehicles.

In the autumn of the year another railroad based event takes place. That one is the Color Tour Train. The Steam Railroading Institute in Owosso brings the Northern Arrow to Kalkaska each October. Passengers board at the

Kalkaska Historical Museum for a round trip excursion through the scenic forests that lasts all day. The trees do their part with leaves bursting with color the whole way. Riders can take pictures, get in a game of Euchre or Cribbage or just kick back with refreshments. It might be the best color tour in the lower peninsula.

If those weren't enough, Kalkaska is also host to the National Trout Festival. The festival kicks off at the Trout Fountain to celebrate the opening of trout season in April. The Trout King and Queen Coronation is followed by a week of trout fishing, clinics and competitions, food, races and parades. This event has been going on for more than 75 years and gets bigger every year.

Believe it or not, there is more. The Kalkaska County Museum is located in the Train Depot building in downtown Kalkaska. This is where passengers board the Color Tour Train. The exhibits are all from local history. Inside is an Elmer Car, hand-made in 1898. Grace Gilbert is remembered here. She was the famous Bearded Lady who traveled with Barnum and Brothers. The history of the lumber era is preserved in the museum as well. Then there is the Cherry Street Market. People on their way somewhere else during the warm months often find themselves startled by the size of this roadside market. It covers nearly a city block and is so awesome that many travelers go just a short way before turning around to go back. Visitors who have been to Kalkaska before almost always have the market firmly in their schedule. The market has the best and most extensive variety of gifts, flowers, veggies and goodies in the north, hands down. One other spot I always have on my list is the Trout Town Tavern & Eatery. They have been wowing the customers for years. Take my word for it, order the white chicken chili, it is simply the best. There is even more, but maybe it's best to leave a few secrets for travelers to discover for themselves.

ONE

PART

OF

LAC

VIEUX

DESERT

IS

A

4,000+

ACRE

LAKE

LAC VIEUX DESERT

Lac Vieux Desert is both a lake, and a region. The name was first applied to the lake by French fur trappers. Lac Vieux Desert is how the translation from the Anishinaabe expression, Gete-gitigaani-zaaga'igan, meaning roughly, "Lake of the Old Clearing" or "Old Garden" came out in French. Not knowing the ancient history of the lake, the river and the Menominee region, the translation misses the essential meaning of the original Anishinaabe by a wide margin. Don't blame the translators. It wasn't the first time there was confusion during translation. They may have been unaware that many words and expressions in Native American languages have both a worldly meaning and a spiritual meaning. They may not have known that the lake is the source of what became known as the Wisconsin River and then the Menominee River that flows through Piers Gorge and on to Lake Michigan at the port of Menominee. The Anishinaabe name for the area refers in part to the extensive rice gardens that were maintained within the lake itself. Gone now, those rice beds, noted by early explorers, have been forgotten by nearly everyone except those whose history and heritage are tied to the area. The gardens were extensive. They were a major source of food all the way down to Lake Michigan where the town of Menominee is today.

There are of islands in the lake and one of them is where a lost secret can be found. If you consult a modern map looking at the northeastern lobe of the lake, you will find a series of islands. Draper Island is usually named on maps, as is Duck Island. Between those, often unnamed, is Near Island. On that island are the remnants of an ancient fort. References can be found to this earthwork on old maps. I first heard about this ancient construction during an Ancient Artifact Preservation Society seminar. At that conference the ancient ruins were attributed to the Hopewell people. The Hopewell are sometimes referred to as the mound builders and flourished from around 100 BC to 500 AD, in the Middle Woodland period. This island is now privately owned and is posted with no trespassing signs. However, in late fall and early winter when the frost has killed the weeds, the outline of the ancient earthworks can be seen from the water.

In prehistoric times this area was a center of travel and trade. Much of that activity was conducted by canoes on the rivers. These weren't small birch bark canoes. These were huge canoes capable of transporting a ton or more of cargo. Some researchers tie these craft to the mystery of the prehistoric copper trade that flourished up the Keweenaw Peninsula, out to Isle Royale and south down the Mississippi River. It is difficult to imagine how much one of these boats could carry until you see one up close, and you can. One of these ancient dugout canoes was discovered underwater near the south end of Thousand Island Lake in 1953. The vessel is made from a single white pine log. It is 32 feet 6 inches long, it's 31 inches wide at the center and is 21 inches high. The walls of the canoe are 1 ½ inches thick. This vessel could transport 15-20 people. Based on the principle of displacement, calculations show that such a dugout could have managed over 4,000 pounds. If a removeable outrigger were added, it would be capable of navigating lakes, even the Great Lakes. With the addition of the outrigger and a small sail, this canoe could have been used to reach a spot as distant as Isle Royale. Archeologists believe the canoe was made by local Indian tribes. The presence of metal bars and oarlocks can be explained. It is thought that lumberjacks found this canoe and added the metal parts. The canoe is on display, with interpretive signs, near the gift shop inside the Lac Vieux Desert Casino.

COPPER CULTURE SPECULATION

A large body of evidence suggests that there was extensive prehistoric copper mining activity on the Keweenaw Peninsula and on Isle Royale. The copper in this area is unique in the world in that it is so pure no smelting is required. Much of the copper could be found lying on the surface and could be worked with simple tools. It seems this prehistoric copper mining continued for a couple thousand years, ending around 1200 BC. The details of this mysterious prehistoric culture have been explored in detail in books and articles. This is a brief sketch of the mystery.

There are prehistoric pit copper mines all over Isle Royale and the Keweenaw peninsula, more than 5,000 of them by some counts. Calculations suggest that at least 500,000 tons of copper were removed from these mines over 2,000 to 3,000 years, perhaps much more. Nothing like this quantity of copper is found in the archeological record in North America. The questions are, who worked these mines and where is all that copper?

One school of thought holds that people came from Europe or the Mediterranean for copper to supply the demand for the bronze age. Since this Michigan copper was so pure it could be worked with tin to produce bronze without the necessity of smelting copper ore. It is speculated that these voyagers arrived in ocean going vessels, loaded them up with copper and returned, a trip that could take up to 3 years. There is evidence that this happened, but there are problems with the theory, a couple are particularly sticky problems. First, there is no evidence of extensive dwellings out on Isle Royale for housing all these sailors and miners. Some people say that they all just housed on their ships while loading the copper. Second, no shipwrecks of these ancient vessels have been found near Isle Royale, the Keweenaw Peninsula of anywhere else in the Great Lakes for that matter. On lakes that are renown for sinking ships, it is odd that none of these European cargo ships sank in two thousand years of shipping copper. Some ancient ships have been found along the coasts of North and South America, but none in the Great Lakes.

Accepting that the mining operations happened, and a massive amount of copper was exported, how was it done with no ruins or wrecks to be found. Perhaps the Lac Vieux Desert canoe holds part of the answer. Given the size, dimensions and displacement capacity of that canoe, it has been calculated that a vessel that size could safely transport 4,000 pounds of men and cargo. A chunk of copper 12 inches square weighs over 550 pounds so, four of those would be over a ton of nearly pure copper. Which means that just one canoe could easily move 1,000 pounds of copper. If there were a fleet of 100 of them, 100 tons could be moved. If the canoe were outfitted with a removable outrigger, it would be stable enough to make the voyage from the Keweenaw Peninsula to Isle Royale. With a fleet of those canoes, both problems are solved.

Each canoe would have a crew of 6 or 8 men to mine and paddle. They would make their way to Isle Royale as soon as the weather permitted, taking a tent and supplies along. Since they are bringing a temporary dwelling, no permanent buildings would be necessary. The men would carry out mining operations with the other crews. If storms blew up, they would simply pull the canoes up on to shore to safety. When enough copper had been mined, they would load the canoe, attach the outrigger, perhaps even a small sail and head for the Keweenaw. Six men would make the journey leaving two behind to continue mining. The six man crew could make the trip in 10 – 12 hours. They would have plenty of daylight in the summer. Upon arriving at the Keweenaw Peninsula, they would unload the copper, get fresh supplies and head back to the island for another load of copper. With a fleet of just 100 canoes each carrying 1,000 pounds of copper and only making 2 round trips per summer, they would move 100 tons of copper to the Keweenaw each season. That is a lot of copper over the centuries. When winter would approach the men would pack up and return home to the mainland taking their tents and possessions with them. They would leave their mines and mining tools behind knowing they would be there when spring came.

So, we have no need of permanent dwellings on Isle Royale and no need for great cargo ships to anchor there, weathering the storms, while waiting for a load of cargo. Since no wrecks have been found along the Keweenaw, what happened to the copper that was taken there? The question is, if no great ships came to get the copper, how did it get to the ocean going vessels waiting at coastal ports. There are several routes, all possible using our fleet of dugout canoes. One would be to transport the copper to Canada instead of the Keweenaw and then overland to the sea. Another would be to use the canoes to move the copper east to the White Fish gap and then down to Lake Michigan where it could be transferred for further transport. Another would be to paddle down the outside of the Keweenaw Peninsula to the Ontonagon River. The fleet would enter the river, go past the Ontonagon Pyramids to their first portage. In two portages they would be on the Mississippi River and the copper would be sent on to the Gulf of Mexico on river boats designed for the purpose. Finally, our canoes could move the copper to Lac Vieux Desert, the source of the Menominee River and then down the river to Lake Michigan. Any of these methods eliminates the need for ocean going vessels to make their way onto the Great Lakes. This could all be accomplished with 100 canoes. Consider what could be accomplished with 500 canoes. The big cargo ships, designed for ocean transport, could simply sail to a given seaport and collect copper. Copper that was mined in previous seasons and transported there in stages by cargo canoe in previous seasons.

LAKENENLAND,

JUNK

ART,

A

FIREPLACE,

AND

A

BOG

TRAIL

????????????

LAKENENLAND

The section of M-28 between Marquette and Au Train
runs along the shore of Lake Superior with beautiful
lakeshore scenery. About midway, opposite that
lakeshore, a huge sign announces an unusual attraction,
Lakenenland, "Junkyard Art". To describe Lakenenland
as a sculpture park is a bit misleading. Dozens of
sculptures are scattered through 37 acres and a nice track
allows access to a everyone. However, these are high
falutin' works that usually come to mind when one thinks
sculpture, you know, like Michaelangelo or something.
No, these works of art are made from tons of scrap metal
collected from sites all over the upper peninsula.

When you pull in you pass a small pond. Past that is the
parking area. Next to the parking area is a large pavilion
with seating and shade. From the parking area you can
enter the sculpture section by walking, driving, cycling,
whatever your preference. The scrap has been
transformed into more than 80 installations that are true
to the region, great fun to see, and in a beautiful wooded
setting. There are depictions you would expect to find in
the far north, like the two giant lumberjacks working a
log with their crosscut saw or the Finnish Dog Sled.
Others are a bit different, a helicopter, a Tasmanian Devil,
a bar band, a UFO, and the ever popular, log with
bowling balls growing out of the North side, where they
always grow in the wild.

There is another special feature of this park. Travel in the upper peninsula involves a lot of driving on two lane roads that run through thick forests. Often, the forest hugs the side of the road and is so dense, you can't see what might be hidden just a short distance inside. At Lakenenland, there is a trail that can provides visitors a glimpse of what parts of that wild forest can be like. Directly across from that pond at the entrance is a gateway, easy to miss it, with a sign that says Bog Trail. If you want a fun walk, take time to follow the trail. It is a short, 1/4 mile, walking only trail, that is scenic and educational. Be aware, the bog trail does go through a woodland and a wetland, expect the usual denizens like mosquitoes and black flies. Always take precautions against ticks and keep pets on a leash.

The first leg of the trail isn't terribly remarkable. Just an undulating pathway through the pines and cedars with some small open viewing areas, a nice easy stroll. Then you come to a sign, just before a plank bridge across a damp area. That plank is a test. The sign cautions that there is a narrow boardwalk ahead and if you have trouble crossing the plank, you should turn back. Heed the warning because in a short distance you will encounter a winding plank boardwalk made of split logs. That log pathway is the return leg of the trail. The planks are only 12 to 16 inches wide, there is no handrail and if you step off you, will be in the bog. If you can manage it, you are in for a treat. The wooden path is raised above the bog by a foot or so and takes you into a swampy area that would ordinarily be inaccessible to all but the most dogged hikers. There are a couple of places where there are benches for a short rest and there are interpretive signs that describe the plant and animal life that inhabit this kind of ecosystem.

After short way along the log pathway, you will see words painted on the log road. Things like, "Bear Cub", "Snow Owl" or "Fox". Pause at each of those spots and examine the area around you. Somewhere in the trees, stumps and wildflowers, will be a silhouette of the animal named. These cutouts are fun as is everything in this park. For instance, when you see the words "Whitetail Deer" it won't be a silhouette of a big buck with a majestic rack that you see. Instead, there will be only the hind end of the deer with the white tail pointed straight up, just like the glimpse of a deer running away that many a frustrated hunter has seen. Be sure to watch for the rubber boots sticking up out of the swamp at one place. They are a nod to the ongoing battle between the creator of this fantastic place and the local bureaucrats who would like to shut the whole thing down.

Lakenenland can also be reached on a snowmobile trail designated as #417. The park is open year-round and during the winter there is often a fire in the fireplace inside the pavilion.

WHERE

FOOD

GROWS

UPON

THE

WATER

MENOMINEE

A visit to Menominee can be a journey back in time, into the history of a unique community where the story of the exploration of Michigan has been preserved. The word Menominee has been translated to mean "wild rice country" or "where food grows upon the waters". These rough translations refer to the wild rice that grew in abundance in these parts. The rice, the waters it grew in and the fish that also inhabited those waters all played key parts in the history of Menominee. The lands along the river were home to both the Chippewa and the Menominee peoples. Upstream from the modern city of Menominee are extensive ancient burial grounds, dance circles and extremely rare raised garden beds indicating how well-developed rice cultivation was before European explorers arrived here. Important as rice production was, the Sturgeon that spawned in the river every spring were just as critical as a food source. So critical in fact, that a war was fought over control of the river. At one point during the sturgeon run, the Menominee dammed the river. This act made it easier to harvest the sturgeon, but it also prevented the sturgeon from getting further upstream where the Chippewa were dependent on the sturgeon after a long winter had made food scarce. The Chippewa decided to fight, and hundreds of Menominee died in the battle. Those fallen were buried at a spot since known as Burial Ground Point. This conflict was also known as the "Battle of the Pierced Forehead".

Some interpretations claim this is a mythical story, intended to illustrate divisions among the tribes.

The Menominee River also played a pivotal role for trappers and explorers coming into the area. Some of that history is preserved at the Chappee Rapids Learning Center, a project of the Menominee County Historical Society. Louis Chappee, a French nobleman, arrived here in the early 1800's and set up his trading post, the first in the region. The site, having been protected from development, appears much as it did when Mr. Chappee arrived. There are giant oak trees and an extensive stand of white birch trees. When you make your way down to the river, the original boat landing site is right there. The landing is also surrounded by huge oak trees and massive old willows. When characters in period costumes act out daily events at the site, you can picture what life must have been like. It is easy to imagine that cargo canoes and other vessels will be coming downstream any moment to land with goods to trade. A simple walking path along the river encourages more exploration. Back up away from the river is a small burial site, fenced off. The headstone marks this as Mr. Chappee's final resting place, here in the wilderness he loved. The Chappee Rapids Learning Center is open to everyone. From the parking lot, a nicely groomed trail leads through the white birches to the historic site. There are only minimal facilities.

It wasn't long before the lumber era caused rapid expansion in the region. At one point, Menominee produced more lumber than any other city in America. The prosperity brought about by the lumbering industries is reflected in the gorgeous historic architecture along the waterfront where the main business district is located. A walking tour of the waterfront includes several historic sites and architecture that is as unique as the history of the town itself. The lumber era was so profitable that the town had enough surplus to invest in the arts. They built the opera house at that time. It is currently undergoing renovation. Another of those historic buildings is the Spies Public Library. In addition to historical documents and normal library activities, the library maintains a rotating exhibit of objects on loan from the historical museum. Many of these will be what is expected, articles of clothing, diaries and personal items. Sometimes the exhibit will include the unusual. On one visit there were two oddities being shown. One was a petrified tongue, yes, a tongue. The other was something I have never seen anywhere else. On a couple of small twigs are the skeletons of some kind of water creature. They look almost like the mechanism seen on a Venus Fly Trap plant. They are white in color and seem to be clinging to the twigs. No one to whom I have shown the pictures have any idea what these are.

The real treasures are in the Menominee County Heritage Museum. The museum is housed in the historic St. John's Catholic Church building now on the National

Register of Historic Places. The church was erected around 1921 and is now a repository of priceless artifacts and rare items from the past. The interior space is packed with exhibits, most of which, are related to local history. One of the first things visitors notice are the breathtaking stained-glass windows. They are huge and the colors are amazing. The windows were manufactured in Munich, Germany and were part of the original construction. There too many objects on display to describe them all. Some noteworthy exhibits include, prehistoric dugout canoes and several objects from the copper culture. There is rare pulp grinder which was misidentified as a grindstone for many years. A large miniature circus is fun when the animation mechanism is turned on. There is a full-size iron lung, one of only five known to exist. Then there is the "Mystery Ship" exhibit. The wreck of the mystery ship was discovered and brought up in the 1970s. Due to a lack of funding for restoration, the wreck languished. The wooden ship was rotting away and disintegrating. A few years after it was recovered the unidentified ship, was bulldozed. The museum has photos, sketches and some of the few remaining artifacts from shipwreck. There is much more to see and the guided tour brings it all to life. A small building next to the church is the M.J. Anuta Research Center. It is a treasure trove of documents. When I was researching the ancient burial grounds and gardens up on the Menominee River, I was only able to provide sketchy details about what I was looking for. The staff was able to locate what I needed out of the thousands of documents, photographs and old maps. The annex is an amazing resource for anyone researching the history of this area.

The attractions and destinations are scattered across Menominee County. I found the help offered by the MENOMINEE COUNTY HISTORICAL SOCIETY to be invaluable. Contact them at P.O. Box 151, Menominee MI 49858 - (906) 863-9000

WANT

TO

RIDE

WITH

THE

HOUNDS

IN

PURSUIT

OF

THE

WILY

FOX

?????????????????

METAMORA

Though I've visited Metamora many times, I still struggle to describe it. It is a small village just a bit north of metro Detroit but may as well be in another world. Everything seems to be different from almost anywhere else you go. It isn't so much that things look different, although they do, it is the focus of the community of 600 people or so that makes the difference. When you get talking with the locals, the conversation is bound to include either the hunt, the horse farms, the trails and nature areas, hot air balloons or, perhaps, wassail.

This is an historic place, but one thing seems to be missing. Most older towns in the south of Michigan have stately historic mansions left over from the lumbering era. Sometimes these old homes are part of an architectural tour or have been converted to a museum. That isn't the case in Metamora. It seems the locomotive kept setting the town on fire. Not sure how factual the story is, but the old timers tell it this way. The train came through town on a regular schedule. There was a steep hill that had to be climbed so it was necessary to shovel a lot of coal into the boiler to get up enough steam to make the grade. One consequence was that hot sparks would be spewed into the air. Some of those sparks landed on the bigger homes and a conflagration would ensue. It happened often enough that most of the stately old homes in town were lost to the flames.

One fact that is not in dispute is the importance of horses in Metamora. As the lumber era ended and manufacturing grew in places like Flint and Detroit, the residents of Metamora expanded their equine activities, and they prospered. The horse is an integral part of life here; the theme repeats all over the area. There are top-flight horse farms in every direction. You can purchase quality tack downtown. Zorka Pondell is a nationally recognized jeweler in town specializing in pieces celebrating the horse. Her shop is even called Classic Horse.

One major event in town is the Metamora Hunt. There are a whole range of events that revolve around the tradition of the sport of foxhunting that has been part of life here for more than nine decades. This is the real deal, pursuing foxes across the fields, through the mists and forests on horseback. Veterans and experienced foxhunters rave about Metamora. Beginners will find a welcoming membership ready to help and instruct. They offer clinics and classes on the sport, what to wear and cross-country riding. There are all kinds of events throughout the year. There is Land Owners Picnic, June Horse Show, Puppy Show, Hunter Trials and a whole lot more.

If you can't participate in the hunt or don't ride, you can take a drive and tour the horse farms. There is the Metamora Hunt Stable Tour every August, or you can just take a drive any time of year. A favorite Horse Country

Drive follows this route: From the center of town go east on Dryden until you come to Barber Road. Go south to Brocker. At this point you can turn west, or continue on to Rock Valley Road, and then turn west there. Travel west until you come to Blood Road, then turn north again and make your way back to town. Essentially it is a big circle. All the way you are cruising through the broad meadows and fields of Metamora's horse country. Beautiful horses, well-kept buildings, and stunning homes are on every side. It is easy to understand how the Metamora Hunt has continued to grow here. It is also easy to forget, that downtown Detroit is less than an hour away.

There are other events that draw visitors to town. The annual Metamora Days festival attract festival goers from across the region. This late summer celebration includes an antique car show, parade, crafters, and the spectacular assembly and launch of colorful hot air balloons. Then there is Wassailing, yet another feature that makes Metamora a different place to visit. It happens December and follows wassail tradition with a horse-drawn carriage parade thrown in. Wassailing can include a number of activities. There is brewing the wassail and mixing in the spices. So, then the spiced beer or mulled wine must be consumed, and Christmas carols sung. Sometimes the singing goes house to house.

It isn't all horsing around in Metamora. Though it is near a major metropolitan city, nature areas are all around the village. The Metamora Hadley State Recreation Area is just a couple miles west of town. Hadley encompasses over 700 acres with a large lake with a boat launch and fishing pier. The park offers over six miles of hiking trails and more than 200 campsites. You don't need to bring equipment, they rent bikes, canoes and kayaks.

If you like your nature experiences to be a little wilder, the Seven Ponds Nature area is also close by, east this time. The nature area has an excellent orientation center for educational purposes. There are seven ponds on the property each with a nature trail. In addition to the trails and ponds there is a well-maintained butterfly garden and guides for bird watching. One quite unique feature is Earl's Prairie. Hundreds of years ago the dense forests ended at wide open prairies of tall grasses and wildflowers. Nearly all those prairies are gone, but you can experience what they were like by walking the trails at Earl's Prairie. The trail will take you on a tour of the incredible diversity to be found in those prairies. There are dozens of specialized plants and flowers, some of which have adapted specifically to the prairie environment. The prairie is another favorite for birdwatching. The road to Seven Ponds is gravel.

No matter what time of year you visit Metamora, you will eventually make your way to the White Horse Inn, right in the center of town. It isn't quite the same as it was for its' first century of operation. The inn has been remodeled and is a source of pride in Metamora. The original part of the structure is over 150 years old, constructed by Lorenzo Hoard. Before the remodeling the inn was said to be haunted by Lorenzo's ghost. Visitors and staff reported hearing heavy footsteps in empty rooms, lights would flicker, trays would fall off tables and a shadowy form appears in an antique mirror. In those days, just after closing, the owner would leave a pair of boots for Lorenzo at the top of the stairs. In the morning, the boots were often in a different spot. Since the remodel, the paranormal events seem to have diminished. The cuisine has only improved and is the talk of the town.

Event dates and times and general updates are available at www.metamorachamber.org.

MILFORD

HOSTS

THE

COLD

BUTT

EUCHRE

TOURNAMENT

EVERY

WINTER

MILFORD

Milford is a village where they have figured it out. After my first visit I started asking people around Michigan if they knew about the town. Nearly every time I mention Milford to someone who has been there, the response is the same. "Yeah, Milford has a beautiful downtown, great place". That downtown district reflects their dedication to an idea. After even a brief visit it is obvious that some real planning was involved. Downtown Milford is as walkable as it gets, and you will want to pause and take in the activity. The downtown shopping district is so unique that some people say, "if you can't find it in Milford, you probably don't need it." There are dozens of shops, galleries and dining establishments and nearly every one of them is locally owned. You won't find any chain stores or franchises here. They've got decor, gifts, apparel, a shoe store, Nana's Niche, toys, art galleries, Native American, candy, sweets and lots of eats. There is more but this will give you an idea, plan to have a full day.

The community has successfully combined quiet residential neighborhoods, a walkable downtown and close in nature areas, into a wonderful getaway destination. The historic architecture has been renovated in an Old-World style. With vintage lighting, lots of trees, planters and unique shops, the word charming comes to mind. The entire downtown area, while on the National Register of Historic Places, is surrounded by lakes, rivers and parks. Milford is pedestrian friendly and dog friendly, in fact, many of the shops put bowls of water on the sidewalk for the puppies all summer long.

There is a lot to do and a lot going on in town. There are several events that take place every year. Some focus on local history and others have to do with the Huron River that runs through Milford. Traditional festivals and events are included like a Memorial Day Parade and fireworks for Independence Day, but there are some different celebrations here as well. Something is going on in every season. There is the Cold Butt Euchre Tournament where competitors sit on blocks of ice. In January and February, it is a tradition to head over to Kensington Park where the black cap chickadees are said to come and eat out of your hand. In spring birdwatchers welcome back the nesting Ospreys. The 1st weekend in June brings the International Kite Festival just down the road. Summer brings the Blind Canoe Race where teams of 3 race on the river. Two paddlers wear blindfolds and one other person, without a blindfold, calls out the directions. The warm months are also the time when the Plein Air Painting event lures all the artists out to the nature areas all around town. Plein air painting is all about getting out of the studio and painting and drawing in the landscape. The artists gather tubes of paint, brushes, canvas and easel and head to a park, pond or river and create works of art. At the Milford event, time allowed for painting is limited as an additional challenge to the artists. In the autumn the Brewed in Michigan festival brings 30-40 craft brewers to town.

In the background for all of this are the beautiful parks, millponds and the Huron River. The ponds, lakes and Pettibone Creek are popular with paddleboard and kayak enthusiasts, but that river may be the favorite trail in the whole area. There are a couple of places to put in, but if you don't have your own canoe or kayak, Heavener's Canoe and Kayak Livery is the place to go. They are experts on the river trail and understand local water conditions. They can help with short floats of a couple hours up to river excursions lasting three days. If you decide to google the Heavener location be aware that the address on Garden Road can be misleading. Driving that road out of downtown Milford will lead to a spot where the bridge is out and has been for years. The best way to get to the Heavener launch is to make your way to the Proud Lakes Recreation Area on Wixom Rd. The Heavener location is inside the recreation area, so you need a Michigan Recreation Passport.

A BIT OF HISTORY

There is so much history has been preserved here that history buffs make this a must visit. Most of it can be enjoyed at the Historical Museum, but there are other attractions as well. The cemetery has a "Potter's Field", there is historical signage scattered around town relating the facts about the impact of the mills and the railroad. There were so many historic homes and factories that the even "privy divers" make Milford a field trip for research. For more about the architecture the Historical Museum has prepared a brochure, Bridging Time - A Walking Tour.

A tour of the Museum provides information about what can be found around town, the historic buildings, locations where events took place and a guide to the historical markers that have been placed in Milford. The tour will also inform and entertain. I visit small town museums all the time and consider this tour as one of the best I have taken. The docents are well informed and bring the exhibits life. At first glance the exhibits don't seem all that unusual. There is a replica of a log cabin, tools and implements, old maps, old furniture, old paintings and old photographs. All of this is to be expected. What sets this museum apart are the stories and details the docents provide. There is furniture brought from Europe, rare in that most pieces didn't survive the shipwrecks and train wrecks. There is the wonderful hobo art, also known as tramp art. Milford is the mid-point on the railroad between Detroit and Saginaw and was a favorite of the hobos. Most hobo activity took place between 1880 to 1940, yet hobos were known to be camping north of town as late as the 1980's. Hobos were usually looking for work or a meal and, in payment for food or a place to sleep, would often craft a gift. Sometimes it was a small carving or a walking stick. Sometimes it was a real work of art like the amazing box displayed in the foyer of the museum. The box is ornately carved and quite complex. The small drawer on the front has a hinged bottom that drops open when the drawer is closed. Anything that was in the drawer drops into the compartment hidden below and can only be retrieved by removing the bottom of the box.

There are a couple dozen very unusual or extremely rare items in this museum including a plow salesman's sample, a blanket that survived the Chicago fire and itinerant art work paintings. The tour explains them all and even teaches the origin of terms like "Gone to Kent" and "sleep tight". I will leave the rest of the treasures for visitors to discover on their own.

SHENANIGANS, BACK IN THE GOOD OLD DAYS

Back in the day, Milford was a bustling mill town, central to a region that was growing quickly. In the 1830's, this was the frontier. A few miles away, a crossroads became infamous as the site of "Bogus Corners". A blacksmith shop at the crossroads was involved in a scheme with counterfeiters. They would fill a box with fake coins and make a visit to a successful local business or farmer. The tale they told was that they had to make a sudden trip East and the silver was just too heavy to take on the stagecoach as luggage. Would the farmer lend them a fraction of the value in paper money and hold the silver as collateral? If the travelers had not returned within a week or two, the lender could open the box and spend the money. This scam worked several times before the blacksmith was jailed and the counterfeiters fled.

Then there were those elections. A nearby community had intense political rivalries. This was a time when some elections were determined by contests in which each side erected a tall pole, the tallest would win the election. In 1876, the Democrats erected a hickory pole, the Republicans went with tamarack. The Democrats were certain of victory after standing a hickory shaft that was 108 feet tall. The Republicans then stood their tamarack and cheering broke out, theirs was longer, by ten feet. The hickory guys were suspicious, and a pole inspection followed. It was revealed that the tamarack was spliced with an extension, 30 feet from the top. This method of determining the outcome of elections was abandoned when all the tall timber had been lumbered off.

The "Best Kept Secrets" project for Milford is sponsored by the Red Maple Retreat B&B. Heavner Nature Connection Canoe & Kayak Rental co-sponsored the project. The Red Maple Retreat is a great lodging option because there is too much to see and do in Milford to get it all in on a day trip. The "Retreat", located in a quiet residential area just 6 blocks from the hustle and bustle of downtown, is a 1950's house that has been lovingly prepared with travelers in mind. This place is peaceful, the tensions of the days journey begins to drain away within minutes of your arrival. It keeps getting better. The house is full of light from the large windows in the sunroom. The thick plaster walls keep out what few sounds there are outside. Every square inch of this house is immaculate in its cleanliness. Everything you could possibly need has been provided.

LITTLE

SWITZERLAND

IS

JUST

NORTH

OF

NEWAYGO

NEWAYGO

There are so many natural wonders scattered across Newaygo County, it could easily be called Michigan's outdoor playground. There is more than one "secret" destination here, but the best kept secret is probably the Coolbough Natural Areas. In this vast nature preserve is one of the few remnants of an Oak Savanna. Now extremely rare, this type of forest was fairly common in the early 1800's. Sometimes they were referred to as a dry sand prairie, oak-white pine barrens or simply an oak opening. The prairie in the Coolbough Nature Area has been restored. White pines and oaks spread their limbs above the open sandy grassland.

A walk through the Coolbough Natural Areas is a great nature experience and is an opportunity for discovery. Hiking the various trail loops reveals unusual topography, rare plant life and ruins of a lost community. Just a few steps from the parking area is a large map that shows the area, the different loops and some of the nature the visitor can expect to find. On my first visit I headed for a feature on the map called the "Valley of the Ants", I just had to find out what that could be. When I reached the first trail junction, I discovered one of the great features in this preserve, the maps. There is a map at each junction showing where you are and what your options are. The maps are essential because this is a big nature area and it would be easy to get confused on the winding trails. The blue trail on the east side of the property is open for hiking and horseback riding. This trail offers views of the East Pond, West Pond and adjoining cattail marshes, as well as some of the prairie and old homestead remnants on the far east side of the CNA. This trail also goes through white pine forest along the north side of the ponds and wetland, and through a mixed forest type on the south side of the wetland. There are several loops ranging from under 2 miles to more than 3 miles. The trails are quite steep in spots and the bridges across the Coolbough Creek are narrow board foot bridges. Some trail areas are open to horses.

The diversity of habitats is one of the features of the Coolbough Natural Areas that makes any visit a day of discovery. Visitors have the chance to explore ponds and wetlands, hike through white pine and white oak forest, search for butterflies and wildflowers on prairies and barrens, and listen to the bubbling waters of Bigelow and Coolbough Creeks. In another part of Coolbough are more unusual features. There are ruins of old farms, now little more than foundations remain. Use caution, there are holes and old wells hidden in the undergrowth. Oddly, there is a patch of prickly pear cactus growing near one of the old homesteads.

A BIT OF HISTORY
To understand why the CoolBough Creek Natural Area looks the way it does, a little historical information will help. In the late 1930's this area was known as The Big Prairie. Accounts from a 1941 WPA project describe the

area as a sandy wasteland of several square miles. At one time this was all forest which was cleared for farmland. These conditions are great for certain grasses and wildflowers but are awful for agriculture. The enormous sand dunes began to form and move. The shifting sand dunes have blotted out trees, houses and fields with a completeness seen only in the "dust bowl" of the plains. They built fences to hold back the sand, but the dunes buried those as well. Finally, restoration efforts were put in place to start reforestation. There is a story of a cemetery at the western edge of this Michigan desert with tombstones from the 1850's.

DIRECTIONS - From Newaygo, take M-37 to Croton Drive (at the intersection immediately north of the Muskegon River). Turn east on Croton and go 3.7 miles to Barberry Avenue. Turn north and go one mile; Barberry will end at 58th Street. Turn east (right) on 58th, which will curve to the north to become Hazelwood. The parking lot is on the corner of 58th and Hazelwood. From Barberry on the roads are gravel.

There are several other nature areas to explore. Two are particularly noteworthy, the Loda Lake Wildflower Sanctuary and Sailors Pines.

The Loda Lake Wildflower Sanctuary is the only wildflower sanctuary inside a National Forest in the United States. Through more than 70 acres and a hiking trail of about 1 1/2 miles you can discover a sampling of wildflowers and plants that used to cover much of lower Michigan. In fact, more than 200 plants have been identified and you can find them easily by following the trail map provided near the trail head. There are numerous informative signs all along the trails to help identify trees, shrubs and flowers. The sanctuary includes a small spring-fed lake, a wetland area, a creek and marshy areas. There is an oak forest, pine plantations and the remains of an old farm site. These ecosystems attract a wide variety of birds. The sanctuary provides a bird checklist that shows more than 120 varieties of birds to be found there. Loda is a gorgeous place for a quiet break or a full day. There is a picnic area and there are rustic facilities. There are no shops or services and it is important to note that you will have to drive a gravel road to get there. This is a National Forest so there is a day fee. The Loda Wildflower Sanctuary is in northern Newaygo county about 6.5 miles north of White Cloud. Go west on 5-Mile Road to Felch Ave. (gravel) and go north. After a bit you will find the gravel drive to the paved parking area.

The Sailors Virgin Pine Forest is a place where you can still walk through a stand of virgin timber in the lower peninsula. In the 1920's the lumber era was coming to an end and Mr. William Sailors was reviewing his timber holdings. He found that he owned a stand that was maturing, but the trees were not yet large enough to harvest. He had participated in the lumber boom and had seen the giant pines toppled forest by forest. Mr. Sailor's decided to preserve this last stand of pines and today you can wander through them and see what lumberjacks would have seen in the 1800's. Some of these are now giants, 30" in diameter and 100' tall. This stand of pines is dedicated to Mr. and Mrs. Sailors. The area is managed by their children. The pines are located on 52nd Street a quarter mile east of Locust Ave out near the Croton-Hardy Dam.

At the center of all this natural beauty, more than 200 lakes and 350 miles of rivers and streams is the City of Newaygo. There are places to eat and a number of shops; there is even a bookstore. At the main intersection just a couple of blocks from the Muskegon River is another important feature, the Newaygo County Museum and Heritage Center. The museum is a major repository of Native American artifacts that tell the story of their culture, their history and way of life. There are several exhibits that depict life in Newaygo during the lumbering era. Included are exhibits that illustrate the impact of the development of the Muskegon River, not the least of which is the Hardy Dam. The dam, a few miles upstream from Newaygo on the Muskegon River, was built in 1931. It is gigantic and is the largest hydroelectric plant in the Lower Peninsula producing enough electricity for a city of 24,000 people. This structure, the largest earthen dam east of the Mississippi River, has turned the upstream part of the Muskegon River into the 4,000+ acre Hardy Dam Pond. The pond has nearly 50 miles of almost undeveloped shoreline including no private

cottages or homes on it. Downstream is the Hardy Dam
Rustic Nature Trail where at times it's so quiet in the
woods you forget all about the generators, power lines
and spillways just upstream.

Newaygo county has so much to offer, some visitors go
with a list to make sure they see everything. There are
way too many to list them all, but some favorites keep
making the grade. The Croton Dam is where the great
salmon run is second to none in Michigan. The High
Rollway on Route 82 is where logs were piled in
towering stacks each winter during the lumber era. At the
spring thaw the logs were sent crashing down to the river
to be floated downstream. The Rollway provides
amazing views of the surrounding area from 200 feet up.
The Wessling Observatory invites visitors to enjoy the
dark skies and a little stargazing using their state-of-the-
art telescopes. Some nature lovers come to take a
relaxing float on the Muskegon River or the White River
in White Cloud. For art lovers there are shows at the
Dogwood Center for the Performing Arts, Artsplace in
Fremont, the Grant Fine Arts Center and the Stage Door
Theatre. Other visitors go just for the festivals. Some of
the most popular festivals include the White Cloud to
Hesperia Kayak Race. The Lumber Festival brings the
best logrollers to compete. The Trail Town Celebration
offers kayak racing, crafts, food and fun. In February
Newaygo has the Dam to Dam Fishing Tournament, one
of the best ice fishing events in lower Michigan.
Fremont, home of Gerber, celebrates those babies every

year.

A BIT OF UNIQUE HISTORY
Ashland College – As late as the 1930's one of the last
folk schools in the United States operated in Newaygo
County. This college had no examinations, no credits, no
lesson assignments, no degrees, no required class
attendance, and no entrance requirements except the
student be at least 18 years of age. The curriculum
focused on life skills with no set course of study. The
school was established by Danish settlers to teach new
immigrants English and to help them learn the skills
needed for living in their new country. Study included
training in recreation, dancing and folk songs, games and
almost any other activity that would help the student
enjoy life.

Some say Newaygo County was named after Chippewa
Indian Chief: Naw-wa-goo, one of the signers of the
Treaty of Saginaw in 1812. One story tells that the word
"Newaygo" is an Indian word that means 'much water'. I
heard a different tale about how Newaygo got its name.
This version suggests that it comes from an English
phrase that got garbled by the Indians. According to this
story, traders visited an Indian village a couple miles
below Newaygo and sold some dishpans to the women
who hung them around their necks as ornaments.
Eventually, the ladies grew tired of the cumbersome
necklaces and stored them away. Then, one winter day,
the villagers were having fun sliding down the slopes on

boards. One of the elder women brought out her dishpan, sat down on it and raced down the hill blowing past the young braves. At last there was a use for all these dishpans and every Indian who had one was soon "dishpanning down the hill". In their exhilaration they would shout in broken English the phrase that later became the name of the sport and finally the Indian word 'Newaygo'.

OF THOUGHT AND REASON

The largest stretch canvas painting in America is on display in Big Rapids, Michigan. At one time "Of Thought and Reason", by artist Robert L. Barnum, was the largest stretch canvas painting in the world. This work of is 130 feet long and 10 feet high equaling 1300 square feet. It took Mr. Barnum 2 years to finish the painting. Just as remarkable as the size of the canvas is the scope of the subject matter. The painting is a visual parable of how knowledge has evolved or the history of learning. There is no other message or meaning intended beyond that. The artist leaves it to the observers to take away what they will.

The painting employs dozens of images to chronicle the discovery and development of knowledge through the ages. The story is told in a sort of chronological order from left to right. The beginning shows a female figure and then a cave scene with people sitting around that all important discovery, fire. More images continue across the canvas including religious symbols, a blind muse, a pen indicating the power of writing, children at play representing discovery. Progress continues along the canvas with images of war, mechanical inventions like the car and the whole thing ends with a depiction of that most improbable of machines, the computer. The very last image at the extreme right is another woman, but this one is much different from the female figure at the beginning of the painting. It is difficult to photograph this painting since it is mounted a curved wall and is 130 feet long. So, the only way to really study the story that is being told is to go there and spend some time in reflection.

"Of Thought and Reason" is on the ground floor of the Flite Library on the campus of Ferris State University in Big Rapids, Michigan. As you make your way to the library, you may notice a number of really big metal sculptures around the campus and the town. These works of art are part of county wide installations of public art. Murals as public art are difficult to create. One reason is that much of modern architecture is steel and glass. It is hard to paint or mount a sculpture on glass, so the artist chose free standing metal sculptures. Most of them are very large, they are made of aluminum or rusted steel and are part of a concept called Aesthetic Engineering. The idea was to bring art back to the public arena. These sculptures developed around idea that art could be more than just pretty. Each of the 14 sculptures is intended to depict the noble side of human thinking as well as tell a story about the locale in which the sculpture is located.

To create the sculptures, all kinds of engineering problems had to be solved. These objects are huge in some cases and must survive Michigan winters, wind, ice, sun and winds of 60 miles per hour or more. One piece, "Flow" demonstrates some of the difficulties that had to be overcome. It is an aluminum mural mounted on a brick wall in Montague. Not only did the artist have to create a giant three dimensional mural, he also had to engineer the brackets necessary to mount the pieces. The handmade brackets had to support the weight of the metal and resist the high winds common near Lake Michigan. In addition, those brackets had to function without damaging the brick of the building which is on the historical register. There are more than twenty of these sculptures in and around Big Rapids and there are several more scattered across the county. The size and number of sculptures, all with the same theme, make this the largest installation of its kind in America. Aesthetic Engineering, and the works of art created through that process, are also the work of Robert Barnum, the artist who painted "Of Thought and Reason".

THE

ONTONAGON

BOULDER

WAS

ORIGINALLY

ESTIMATED

TO

WEIGH

FIVE

TONS

ONTONAGON COUNTRY

Ontonagon Country, just the saying the words fires the imagination with images of mysterious forested mountains, ancient abandoned mines, roaring waterfalls, lighthouses on the breathtaking Lake Superior shoreline and legendary shipwrecks. At the base of the Keweenaw Peninsula, the Village of Ontonagon is the gateway to the Porcupine Mountains and the natural wonders of Ontonagon Country. Sited at the mouth of the Ontonagon River on Lake Superior, Ontonagon is an outdoor lovers' paradise and a dream come true for history buffs.

A stroll through town gives a glimpse of life in the upper peninsula. It is worth it to take the Walking Tour offered by the Ontonagon County Historical Society Museum. The history of the village is revealed through stories and visits to historic structures and the vintage photographs of old Ontonagon posted all over downtown. The shops, dining and art are an integral part of life on the shore of the Gitchee Gumee. An absolute necessity is a visit to the Historical Museum. This is where visitors can acquire brochures describing attractions across the region and schedule a tour of one of the three lighthouses that served this port. Plan to spend time inside the museum. The number and variety of exhibits can be a little overwhelming. Here, the history of the lumber era, the copper mining era and maritime activities are on display. The friendly staff members add to the experience with intimate knowledge and entertaining storytelling.

As cool as a walk through the village can be, the surrounding countryside is filled with fun destinations and natural wonders that will fill several days. The area can easily be explored via hiking trails, water trails, snowmobile trails as well as roads. In fact, Ontonagon is famous as the starting point for over 500 miles of trails that crisscross the region. As well-known as the area is to nature lovers, there is one trail that is unique in Michigan and yet, is almost unknown outside the immediate area. Just outside of town is the Township Campground on the shores of Lake Superior. The campground has great campsites on the lakeshore and off. It has a wilderness trail for those seeking solitude in the forest and is a good launching spot to explore the little-known Ontonagon Water Trail. The water trail hugs the shoreline in both directions from the campground. At one end of the trail are the ruins of an abandoned lighthouse at Misery Bay. At the other end, off Mineral Point is a shipwreck, the Panama. Along the way are two other lighthouses, the 4 Mile Rock and several rivers. For the adventurous, the Ontonagon River skirts the edge of town. For those who want a river experience but want to avoid wild water, there is the Firesteel River. The current is so gentle that it is perfect for amateurs and those with special needs. If you don't want paddle all the way, there are launch points on the Firesteel and the Flintsteel Rivers out the Lakeshore Dr. to 10 Mile Road. The water trail can be accessed from 13 different launch sites. The Village also maintains a paddle craft landing on Rose Island in the Village where kayakers and canoe buffs can store their vessels while visiting the historic downtown.

SCENIC DRIVE

Visitors and residents alike make their way to the
Porcupine Mountains during peak color season when the
leaves set the hills ablaze for color tours. That tour
usually includes a stop to drink in the view of the Lake of
the Clouds and, perhaps, a drive along the south
Boundary Road to visit the waterfalls at the western end
of the Porkies. As beautiful as these places are, there is
much, much more to be enjoyed in both summer and
autumn. You could just go on a random drive, but
following this route will lead to great scenery, fun
destinations and a stunning scene at the end in both green
seasons and color time.

The Ontonagon Color Tour begins in town. Maps of the
county are available at the Historical Museum. Take M-
38/M-26 toward Mass City. The scenery will be as "up
north" as it gets. Approaching Mass City, watch for signs
leading to the Adventure Mine. Without getting into
details, suffice it to say that this place offers an authentic
mine experience. A hard hat and light are required. Stout
footwear and a jacket will really come in handy. The
mine offers tours into areas that were inaccessible just a
few years ago, and once per year, a mountain bike race
passes through a section of the mine.

From Mass City follow M-26 to Rockland just a few
miles south and west. Rockland is little more than a

crossroads, but there are treasures to be discovered while enjoying the ride. There are three spots of note in town. The Rockland Historical Museum tells the local story including the fact that the first telephone line in Michigan was strung here. Henry's Inn is a place the snowmobile crowd knows well. If the magnificent mahogany bar could talk, it would have tales to tell. Then there is the old Rockland Depot, formerly the First National Bank of Rockland. It is a two-story structure, painted red. It is now a general store and a place to get coffee or ice cream. Inside is a special feature, the Spice Vault. The vault is real, a feature from the old days. Inside, are exotic spices, many in bulk, from all over the world. The proprietors can explain the uses of items that are so unusual you may never have seen them before.

Back on the road, watch for the signs pointing the way to the restored ghost town of Old Victoria. Old Victoria is an historic mining camp, restored to its original glory by the Society for the Restoration of Old Victoria. Tours are offered during the season. Regardless of whether the ghost town is open, the road out there is one of the most spectacular drives in all of Ontonagon Country. In the color season, it rivals the best anywhere.

Back in Rockland, the drive continues south on Route 45 past Bruce Crossing to Paulding. This is the way to the rightly famous Bond Falls. The roads are paved all the way, you can nearly drive right up to Bond Falls in any season. From the parking lot, there are pathways and boardwalks that take one all around the falls and up above them. Bond Falls is the most famous but there are others nearby. Kakabika Falls is more remote but is a roaring cataract during the spring thaw. Agate Falls is close by with an awesome view from atop a railroad trestle, 200+ feet up.

Back north of Bruce Crossing on Route 45 is a small sign, O Kun De Kun Falls. This one requires some work, like a hike of more than a mile. However, when the water is flowing, you can actually walk around behind the falls. Sometimes one wants to get out of the car and just enjoy the view. A great spot for that is the Robbins Pond Road just south of Paulding. That is also the spot where one can watch for the Paulding Light to appear after dark.

Back at Bruce Crossing the scenic tour heads west on Route 28. The drive passes through Ewen of lumbering era fame and takes the visitor to the crossroads of Matchwood. There may not be a sign announcing Matchwood, so watch for the road sign for the Norwich Road. Take the Norwich Road north back toward Lake Superior. The road is narrow and winding, but it is paved. Drive through the farmlands and hunting camps as the road goes. About halfway to the northern end comes the reward, the Norwich Bluffs. After rolling through farmlands and white birch forests, the bluffs suddenly appear straight ahead. The cliffs tower hundreds of feet in the air surrounded by hardwood forests. It may be the best sight in the whole drive.

There is a trailhead where you can park and hike around a bit. There are mining ruins here and prehistoric copper mining pits. The view from atop the bluffs defies description.

Drive on north until the road stops at Route M-64. Take a left and reach Silver City, go south on Route 64 to find the beautiful Bonanza Falls. Go straight and find Scott's Superior Cabins where I like to take my rest. Go right and you will be back in Ontonagon in just a few minutes. Another spot that is a rewarding side trip is the drive around Lake Gogebic. It is the largest inland lake in the upper peninsula, famous for fishing and beautiful color. The lake is adjacent to Bergland just a few miles west of Matchwood.

Ontonagon Country is Copper Country. European explorers began to hear stories of copper deposits in the area while they were still far to the east. The details were so unbelievable that the immense copper deposits described were put down as legend. The stories about the "Ontonagon Boulder" were put down as mythical at best. However, the stories were true and as to the amounts of copper readily at hand, they fell far short of the reality. That reality began to come to light in 1667 when a French missionary, Father Dablon, was guided up the Ontonagon River to a boulder of pure copper weighing in at nearly 5,000 pounds. The copper that made up the boulder was so pure that it required no processing. Enormous as the boulder was, it was little more than the tip of the iceberg. (The Ontonagon Boulder is in the Smithsonian Institute at Washington D.C. but a replica can be seen at the County Historical Society Museum.)

It turned out that copper had been mined in the area, up the Keweenaw Peninsula and out on Isle Royale since 3,000 B.C. or longer. There are thousands of prehistoric pit mines across these regions. Some calculations estimate that millions of pounds of copper were mined and removed prior to 1,000 B.C. when the activity suddenly stopped. I cover the theories about the prehistoric copper culture in other writings. For more information while in the area, make your way to that excellent Historical Museum in Ontonagon that I keep going on about. Another source of historical information is the archives of the Ontonagon Herald, just down the street from the museum.

As cool as all this is, many plan their visit to Ontonagon Country to correspond with one of the festivals that go on throughout the year. There are a dozen and more to choose from. In the spring is the Lake Trout Classic. This tournament takes place the third weekend in May and attracts teams from all over the country and Canada. It aids the Ontonagon County Cancer Association. On the third weekend in July it is Copper Fest. Three days of celebration mark the copper culture with street vendors, fireworks, log rolling demonstrations and more. In the autumn many visitors come for the Color Tours. Mother nature sets the date for this one, but many times the second week of October is a safe bet.

When I choose to not camp, I like to stay at Scott's Superior Inn & Cabins. The accommodations are comfortable, reasonable and centrally located at 22554 Lakeshore Road west of town toward the Porkies. Don & Kathy see to every detail and can answer any question you can come up with about what to see, where to shop and where to get the best pasties. Just wait until you see the two mounted black bears in the lobby.

SECRET PASSAGE

You just never know where or when you will discover one of the best kept secrets in Michigan. We were sitting around the lounge at the Nahma Inn when two couples at the next table started talking an upcoming trip to Saginaw. I couldn't remember the last time I heard people saying how they just couldn't wait to visit Saginaw. So, I excused myself and asked what all the excitement was about? Their response, "Just wait until you tour the Castle and go through the secret passage. If you are a history nut, you're going to love it". So, I began to plan a trip to Saginaw to find out for myself.

It turns out there is an historic structure downtown that has every resemblance to a castle with high walls, towers and turrets. There isn't a moat because the Castle was modeled on a French chateau. The architecture was chosen to honor the early French settlers of the Saginaw Valley. The design was French, but the turrets were meant to represent a frontier fort. This was considered the western frontier when the building was erected in the 1890's. It was to be a federal post office. The castle survived demolition twice. In the 1930's the federal government was considering the construction of a new facility. The community opposed the plan and the "castle" was enlarged. Three decades later another demolition plan came up and again the community saved the "castle". In 1972 it was added to the National Register of Historic Places. The Historical Society of

Saginaw County took over the building in 1979 and it became the Castle Museum.

Anxious as I was to get inside and explore, I did pause to admire that architecture. This is a beautiful building. The style and techniques of the construction would be a challenge today. Just finding the artisans who possess the necessary skills would be a challenge. Inside at last, I went off without a guide or map to see if I could locate the door to the secret passage. I hardly noticed the exhibits as I dashed around the enormous museum. Of course, one thing that makes secret passages so charming is that they are, well, secret. I couldn't find the entrance and never would have without help.

I sought that help and was lucky to meet Mr. Jonathan Webb. He listened to my story and was only too happy to act as guide and guide he did. I didn't know at the time that he was President and CEO and I didn't know that I was going to get a grand tour. The mad dash to the secret passage became a stroll through the history of Saginaw County. Impatient as I was, the tour was very entertaining.

The first stop was to check out the 1914 Saginaw Cycle Car. This one is in excellent condition. The car was first manufactured by the Valley Boat Engine Company. There were many small car manufacturers around Michigan in those times. This vehicle had a feature that set it apart from other cars. The front axle was installed in such a way that after going around a corner, the driver could take his hands off the steering wheel and the front wheels would straighten automatically. Only 35 Cycle Cars were manufactured. The vehicle originally sold for $395.00. I don't think they make them like that anymore.

In the same great hall where the Cycle Car is displayed, there is a larger than life statue of Lady Justice. There were four of them at one time, atop the county courthouse. That building didn't survive demolition and the four statues were lost. This one turned up in a field in rough condition. The statue survived the elements because it is made of zinc, still it is too fragile for restoration. In nearby galleries are extensive exhibits covering the history of the 45 coal mines that operated in Saginaw County, the history of the lumber era is illustrated with a sculpture of a tree that demonstrates the huge size of the forests. After we checked out a few more exhibits, Mr. Webb started leading me toward the back of the museum where he would divulge the location of the secret passage.

On the way, we passed through a room where there was a temporary exhibit that was as remarkable as anything I saw that day. There were interpretive signs and old photographs around the room. In the center under a spotlight was a small machine. It had an odd appearance, was complex and like nothing I had ever seen. There were spindles and pulleys and cogs on wheels. Clueless I checked the sign nearby. It read, Sock Knitting Machine, this machine is one used by the Frankenmuth Woolen Company. That company made 66,000 pairs of socks for the soldiers who fought in WWI. It may not sound like a great discovery, but it led me to that Woolen Company which is covered in another chapter in this book.

There is a secret passage and you can visit it. The passageway is on the second floor and is from days when the "Castle" served as a post office. The passage is painted black and has very narrow slits along one wall at about shoulder height. Peering through any of those slits one is looking down on a large well lit room. That room was used to sort incoming mail for delivery to local addresses. A Postal Inspector would use the passage to keep a surreptitious watch on the mail sorters working below. The idea was to deter theft. The employees knew the observation passage was there, however the Postal Inspector had a private entrance to the building so employees were never certain when he was on the premises and watching. The passage goes all the way around the room so every angle could be covered. The secret passage was worth effort and added fun to a great tour of a museum that has many other secrets to be discovered.

STURGEON WATCH

Sturgeon have had a rough time of it. Once plentiful, sturgeon became so rare that many people had never seen one. They have been described as living dinosaurs or prehistoric survivors. It is estimated that they have been around for more than 130 million years. They grow to enormous size and can live for a century. These giant fish had been harvested almost to extinction. First, they were killed as a nuisance because they would get caught in such numbers that they damaged commercial fishing gear on the Great Lakes. In the 1860's they were killed or dumped back in the lake. In other cases, they were fed to pigs, used as fertilizer and even stacked to be used as fuel for steamboats. Later their meat and eggs became valuable and those same commercial fishermen targeted the Sturgeon. In the 1890's the annual haul from the Great Lakes exceeded 4 million pounds per year. These huge harvests combined with the damage to spawning streams from agriculture and lumbering led to a catastrophic decline in the sturgeon population. Today, 19 of the 20 states within its original range list the sturgeon as protected or endangered.

While the protected status has helped, sturgeon are still rare, but there is a way for anyone to not only see huge sturgeon in the water, you can also interact with them. That opportunity has become available to everyone thanks to the vision and dedication of one woman, Brenda Archambo, President of Sturgeon for Tomorrow.

In northeast Michigan lies Cheboygan County. In the forest there is Black Lake and the Black River, where sturgeon have not only survived, they are thriving, their numbers increasing year by year. Every spring in April and May, those sturgeon move from the lake, up the river to spawn in the waters where they were born, just as they have for thousands of years. During those weeks, the sturgeon are at risk to poachers who covet their eggs as caviar. Individuals and groups can volunteer to keep watch in cooperation with Sturgeon for Tomorrow and the DNR. In the process people can get up close and personal with these freshwater giants.

Sturgeon for Tomorrow coordinates the whole thing. Hosts are camped on the high bluffs above the Black River. Some hosts are there for as long as six weeks. Groups like the Boy Scouts arrive to help on some weekends. Individual volunteers camp in remote spots along the spawning run to ensure that poachers are thwarted. Then there are those amazing students from MSU who work every day to catalog and tag as many sturgeon as possible. In one stretch of the river are 5 or 6 holes where the sturgeon congregate. Divers go in and capture the sturgeon in hand nets. They bring the fish to the bank of the river where students wait to weigh, measure and tag each one. These students are tough. They sit there in the weeds and the mud and the mosquitos and the ticks, working in cold water, 40 to 60 degrees cold. They do this every day for 6 to 7 weeks, as long as the spawn continues. On one morning, we watched the divers bring up more than 30 sturgeon from the first hole alone. It took more than 2 hours and there were 5 more holes to go. They work nonstop, calling out the measurements back and forth to ensure accuracy. As soon as they finish with one, there is another handed up for processing, on and on it goes. Then again, there are days where the sturgeon just don't show up. None the less, the conservation guys and the students are there, in that chilly water, searching and tracking. The sturgeon don't just lay there waiting for the net. They are elusive and will fight with great strength to escape once captured. A six foot sturgeon can weigh in at sixty pounds, most of it muscle from swimming against swift currents for fifty years. Protecting the sturgeon to the point where they can begin to grow in numbers is a major undertaking. For one thing, sturgeon don't begin to spawn until the age of 20. Then there is the troublesome eight day gestation period on fertilized eggs. The Sturgeon for Tomorrow program has produced so much data that other nations draw on it for knowledge.

On the weekend I camped as a volunteer I was made welcome and given a tour of possible campsites from which to choose. The sturgeon were fairly active and we got to see a lot of them. Day visitors were welcome as well and were shown every courtesy by the hosts and Conservation officers. Other groups participate in this conservation effort. On one day, a class of 5th graders from Alpena arrived with a one year old sturgeon that they had raised in their classroom. They were going to release it back into the river where it had been spawned. This was no haphazard undertaking. The students had to keep the baby, named Stu, alive all year and keep him in water from the river. Sturgeon have a keen sense of smell and navigate to the proper place in the river using that sense. They even had to match the temperature in Stu's container with the temperature of the river water on that day, to avoid shock. At the release, there was Brenda Archambo, giving instruction and encouragement.

Camping conditions vary. Though mostly primitive, there is a campground where the hosts and others with campers gather. There are also spots where only a tent will do, since there is no way to get a camper in there. Regardless of which the volunteer chooses, the wilderness is beautiful, the wildlife abundant and the dark skies are full of stars. My small tent site was visited by sturgeon and beaver in the river, ducks, geese and eagles above the river and deer, racoons and foxes along the river. This is a wilderness with predators. Follow instructions for storing food and supplies. I have never heard of a "fun" encounter with a hungry bear.

Sturgeon for Tomorrow also runs the annual Shivaree, the only time sturgeon can be speared in Michigan. The event is tightly controlled requiring the cooperation of the Michigan DNR, and those all important volunteers. Depending on the year, the spearing season will last from 10 minutes to just over an hour. In 2018 the season limit was 7 fish and the season lasted around 19 minutes.

TELEPHONE MUSEUM

Collectors and experts love to use terms such as "one of a kind" or "historic" or "incredibly rare" when describing items found in attics or stored in out of the way museums. Sometimes it's true, sometimes it is mostly true and sometimes there is nothing worth talking about. In the "it's true" category is a museum that can legitimately use terms like "historic" or "incredibly rare". The Telephone Museum in Montrose really does have several one of a kind items, extremely rare objects and some of the largest specific category collections in the world. The museum is a town museum, genealogy center and a telephone museum. Yep, it is almost all telephones, but you have never seen anything like this.

In a world that is increasingly digital in nature, the analog and mechanical objects on display can be puzzling. For the very young, digital citizens, who have never seen a dial phone or lived in a world without Facebook, a trip to Montrose will be long remembered. Consider the legendary string phone, you may have played with them as a child. The classic set up was two empty tomato soup cans connected by a length of kite string. You would punch a hole in the bottom of each can and feed the string through from the bottom into the inside of the can. Then you would tie a shirt button, filched from your Mom's sewing kit, to each end of the string. When pulled taut, that string would transmit sound. Your little brother would hold one can to his ear, and you could yell at him through the opening in the other can. It works. These toys were based on real appliances, string phones were some of the first in use. String phones would work at distances of a mile or more when manufactured with the proper earpieces and wire instead of string. A string phone was one of the first telephones in Michigan, it was installed in St. Ignace. That is just one of the rare objects on display in Montrose.

Just a few years after the string phone, technology had progressed to the point where the "Stoger Step Switch" was in common use. Basically, it worked like this. You would enter a phone booth and dial a number. As you dialed each number, a switch system would identify that digit and set the switch. When all of your digits had been dialed, the "step switch" would send the signal to the phone down the line that matched those numbers. At the Montrose facility they have a working Stoger Step Switch. Watch as someone dials a phone located inside a real live phone booth. The switching system sits next to the booth and you can watch the switches identify the digit and light up the number on a screen. When all the numbers have been dialed, a phone on a stand nearby will ring and someone can answer the call.

Beyond those two examples, there are thousands of antique phones and associated items on display. So many in fact that it is a good idea to take the guided tour. A popular exhibit with many visitors is the collection of "character" phones. These were a departure from the utilitarian black bakelite phones of the 50's and 60's. These were fun. There are superhero phones, Disney character phones and heroes from the old west. Easily the hands down favorite is the animated Tasmanian Devil phone. His ring tone is hilarious. These are all part of the largest public display of "character" phones in America.

It can take a while to see all the exhibits on display. The variety alone can be daunting. The progression of phone designs from those string phones to primitive crank phones to the dial phone to early digital phones and beyond fills a couple of rooms. Among those items is an example of a Hush-A-Phone. This device wasn't a permanent attachment, it was just slipped on and off the mouthpiece of a phone as needed. Advertisements described it as a "voice silencer" designed to reduce sound interference and improve privacy. Hush-A-Phone was sued by the Bell Telephone Company. Hush-A-Phone argued its importance as an aid to privacy and noted that the device improved the clarity of the transmission. They won that landmark case which figured into the eventual breakup of the Bell System.

There are all manner of related devices on display. There is an early answering machine that depended on a reel-to-reel tape machine inside to record messages. Another item is an explosion proof phone designed for use in underground mines. Telephone lines need maintenance. On display is a phone line tester used to test for line integrity. It depended on a telegraph key to send a sound down the line to test it. This tester, a Type L Mathews Woodpecker Telefault, is the only one in existence with an instruction booklet. Dozens of glass insulators are lined up on one wall. A display case shows several styles of dialers. These are small stylus type items used to dial rotary phone dialers so secretaries wouldn't break their nails dialing all day in the course of their employment. The museum houses the largest collection of Phone Pioneer pins in the world, commemorating the countless hours of volunteer work donated by Telephone Pioneers.

Along with the phones, the museum preserves important artifacts in the story of Montrose. One room, houses exhibits that recreate scenes and businesses from the past. The hardware store is there, and the dentist. There is a full display of rare scooters including one that had a ratchet drive. In a corner of that room is an original safe from the old bank. The story is told that it is sitting on the spot where it was placed upon delivery to the museum. After a couple of attempts at moving the heavy safe, it was decided that it was perfect where it was, and the bank display was built around it. One item that is easy to overlook is a book, The History of Milford Township; just one more extremely valuable object preserved here. It is estimated that there are only 30 of these books in existence.

There is more to see; visitors won't be disappointed. The Telephone Museum in Montrose is remarkable not only for the exhibits, but also for the people who make it all possible. The museum is manned by volunteers and is endowed by the Wyman Jennings Foundation, the major supporter. The Montrose Telephone Museum is at 144 East Hickory St. Montrose, MI. 48457

There is one more exhibit that is worth taking the time to visit. It isn't at the museum. It is located in Barber Memorial Park. There you will find a small building in the shape of an octagon. That is where you find the Veterans Bell Memorial. In 2005 Charlie Emmendorfer wanted to honor the service of all U.S. Military Veterans. He decided on a bell and went to work with his crew. They designed and built a stainless steel bell, about 6 feet tall, that weighs in at 4,000 pounds. The building was hand made as well. Volunteers cut fallen ash trees into beams and posts. Wall boards and doors were made locally. The memorial has several exhibits and honors veterans from all over America.

THE

MAP

TO

THE

UNDERGROUND

RIVER

IS

AT

THE

PURPLE

STORE

UNDERGROUND RIVER

Unspoiled natural wonders can still be found up in northeastern Michigan. The rate of development has been much slower there. Wilderness and clean flowing rivers await the visitor who is looking for a getaway that isn't focused on wineries. This day trip revolves around a place in the forest where an underground river bubbles from a hillside. The getaway includes visits to Ocqueoc Falls, the Sink Holes, the big Steering Wheel, the Jolly Dutchman for a burger, walking trails and more. These destinations are scattered across several miles, so a map can come in handy. The first time I went to visit these sites I planned it out carefully. I made up a cooler with water and sandwiches and printed a copy of the simple map on the Michigan Back Roads website. I headed to Onaway and parked within sight of the big steering wheel. The plan was to have a snack and consult my map. It was at that moment that I discovered that both cooler and map were still sitting in my kitchen, swell. Fortunately, I knew of another map north of town on M-211 at the Purple Store. The shop is actually named the M-211 Market, inside is a beautiful map of the area on a chalkboard done in colored chalks. The map shows some destinations that may not show up on navigation devices. Ken & Lois who run the store welcome visitors who want to take a photo of the map to use in getting around.

When I first heard about the underground river, I imagined being inside a great mystical cavern and wandering through stalagmites and stalactites, my torch spluttering in the darkness. I spent a couple hours stumbling around the forest trying to find a cave entrance to the "great underground river". Finally, a kindly local took pity and explained it all to me. No, there isn't a mystical cavern to explore. However, there are places where the river disappears underground and reappears on the surface some distance away. On a quiet day there are spots where you can hear the river flowing underground. Some people even tell of seeing trout and salmon come swimming out of the hillside.

The Underground River is a branch of the Little Ocqueoc River. You could consult the chalkboard map or, follow M-68 east from Onaway, Michigan about 10 miles and turn left on Silver Creek Trail. This is a gravel road. About a mile down the trail will be an unmarked turn-out that is easy to miss. Watch for a sign Silver Creek Trailhead Parking.

OCQUEOC FALLS

Ocqueoc Falls is the largest waterfall in the lower peninsula of Michigan. The word "ocqueoc" comes from the French for "crooked waters". The name fits. The Ocqueoc River does in fact, wind all over in its course across the karst formations in Presque Isle county. Size is only one of the unique features of this waterfall. One of its best features is that it is easy to get to. In fact, this may be the only universally accessible waterfall in the United States. The parking lot is only a few yards from the falls. This is not a big plunge falls, like many in the upper peninsula, it is more an extended cascade with the greatest of three drops being only about 5 feet or so. The gentle angle of the falls and its proximity to the picnic area make this a very popular wilderness swimming spot.

Upon arrival, some visitors head right to the falls. Others stop and visit with the kid in the hot dog costume for a quick snack. Another option at Ocqueoc Falls is to take a hike along the Ocqueoc Bicentennial Pathway. The pathway has groomed winter trails and summer hiking trails. There are several loops. The first is the shortest and, some say, most scenic. The remnants of an old mill race can be seen just above the falls. The trail takes visitors through a beautiful area of the river valley that is forested by towering pines and hardwoods. The trail is usually in good shape and is shared with mountain bikers.

A BIT OF HISTORY

Ocqueoc Falls is on the Ocqueoc River which flows north to Lake Huron at Hammond Bay. The story is told that the mouth of the river was the site of a Chippewa tribal ceremony for the disposition of the crippled and aged. These individuals would rise, at the height of the ceremonial feast, and jump to their death in the waters of the river where it enters the bay.

SINK HOLES

A visit to the sinkholes and a walk along the pathway through the area is not only a different experience, but is also the best way to understand the effect of the karst geology of this entire region. The term karst refers to a topography that forms when soluble rocks like limestone dissolve in water. This action creates underground cavities which may collapse resulting in sinkholes. The sinkhole area is quite extensive with several sinkholes, some of which are lakes like Shoepac Lake and Francis Lake. One or two of those lakes will have water levels that rise and fall from season to season and year to year. The sinkholes are deep, 150 feet deep and more. A walk on the trail and stops on the viewing platforms can give a three-dimensional view of these unusual formations. One of the odd features of the sinkholes is why some have water and others don't. For instance, the bottom of the first sinkhole along the path is more than 100 feet lower than the surface of Shoepac Lake, yet it is dry. Several other sinkholes are dry, and you can climb down but remember you must also climb back up. These are deep and steep. This is very different nature area and is unimproved for the most part. Last time I was there the going was rough and the stairs were in poor repair with railings being quite wobbly.

It is worth the effort to get there if you want to see some real Michigan wilderness. The roads are very good all the way to the actual trailhead and there is decent parking. You can spend a lot of time here and so remember that there are no amenities. The road to the sinkhole viewing area is CO Road 634 or Tomahawk Lake Highway. Go south out of Onaway or north out of Atlanta on M-33.

Go east on Tomahawk Lake Hwy. and north to Shoepac Lake. The trailhead is to the right.

AROUND ONAWAY

Passing through the City of Onaway you may notice the sculptures that abound like the big steering wheel and the giant sturgeon. The steering wheel commemorates the days when the local slogan was, "Onaway Steers the World". This comes from the former industry that made wooden steering wheels, and before that, wooden bicycle wheels. In 1926 a fire broke out in the factory. In a few hours the factory had gone up in smoke and local prosperity with it. Some of that prosperity has returned thanks to Moran Iron Works. They have created the metal sculptures around town and a park where the Wood Rim factory used to be with walkways, sculptures, and informative signs.

The sculpture of the sturgeon reminds travelers of the remarkable work done at Black Lake by an awesome organization, Sturgeon for Tomorrow. Through their unceasing efforts the sturgeon population in the Black River and Black Lake water system has been revitalized. The group works with the DNR to maintain a hatchery and to assist with the spawning run every spring as described in the Sturgeon Watch chapter in this book. The group also works with the DNR in conducting the Shivaree every winter.

ONAWAY STATE PARK

Nature lovers who want to stay over should check out the Onaway State Park. The park is on 150+ acres on the shore of Black Lake. It has a popular 3 mile hiking trail through a diverse set of ecosystems.

ZEELAND

It would be difficult to describe a road trip to Zeeland without understanding their history. While modern day Zeeland has festivals and fun all year long, Zeeland is a place where the traditions and values of the past still run deep in everyday life. When you drive into Zeeland on an early spring day when the trees are in bloom and flower beds are popping, or in any season for that matter, it's easy to see that it isn't all history in this beautiful town. Downtown is vibrant, the shops beckon, the dining spots are busy and there may very well be a festival in progress. Zeelanders have always been proud of their work ethic, Herman Miller is here, and they are just as proud of the celebrations and rewards of that work.

The Zeeland Historical Society diligently preserves the history, and the artifacts that illustrate that history, while Zeeland itself continues to evolve to meet the opportunities and challenges of modern life. Settlers from the Netherlands arrived in the mid 1800's and established the community. The historical museum, housed in the 1876 Dekker Huis home, is right downtown. The hardships and triumphs of those settlers and their descendants are preserved in the exhibits inside the museum. The Historical Society also maintains the New Groningen Schoolhouse. The schoolhouse served as a rural school in the area in the late 1800's.

The museum and old schoolhouse aren't the only

attractions in and around Zeeland, after all, Lake Michigan is only about a twenty minute drive. Just outside of town is the Upper Macatawa Natural Area where the trails are favorites of bikers, hikers and runners. The forests and grasslands of the Upper Macatawa are home to diverse plant life and wildlife. The park includes an extensive wetland that attracts a wide range of birds. The bike path connects to the Fred Meijer Trail and thus to Kent County. Another favorite of locals and visitors is the Critter Barn where one can learn about and interact with a variety of farm animals. Young people can improve their skeet shooting at the Wobble Trap. It is found at Blendon Pines Gun Club. The Wobble is set up to launch clay pigeons along one line until your aim improves. When that happens, it will start launching them in different directions to test your new skill.

No matter what brings visitors to Zeeland, they are invited to "Feel the Zeel". One way to feel it is to come for one of the festivals that seem to be happening in almost any month of the year. In February it is Plaiderday. This when everybody dons their finest plaid and goes downtown for the Chili Crawl. Past years have seen upwards of a dozen homemade chili recipes to sample. The event includes special sales and live music. In April there is the Dutch Dance Event and a student Art Exhibit. In June it is Cycling the City, a group ride through the streets and paved pathways of Zeeland, with summer treats at the end. July has Zeelmania. They don't all become manic, it's a healthy-living street-fair. In August the chalk artists get to work downtown for Chalkfest. September has the Fall Peddlers Market, an open-air lifestyle market with one-of-a-kind vendors peddling everything from antiques to architectural salvage to farm to table treats. Crowds of people arrive in Zeeland to see the one of a kind items offered for sale. These are just a few. There are galas, parades and pumpkins. They may be a little old fashioned over in Zeeland, but they do know how to show visitors a good time. Even the Dekker Huis Museum gets in on the act a few times each year.

There is yet another reason to head to Zeeland, even if it is only for an hour, the burger quest. I am always on the hunt for great burgers and get tips from people all the time. Once in a while they are right, but usually not. Years ago, I stopped at Frank's in downtown Zeeland and was delighted. My burger that day was among the best I have found in Michigan. It was big, it was juicy and it was delicious. When I stopped on a trip in spring 2019 that burger was still great. Frank's Restaurant has been doing it just right for over 90 years.

Vic and Anna Van Deventer, who helped make this chapter possible, operate the Baert Baron Mansion, a significant Victorian Landmark of the 19th century, as a Bed and Bbreakfast. When you see it, you may just want to extend your visit to Zeeland for a couple days. The Baert Baron Mansion reflects the history of bygone days.

Guests may want to lounge on the comfortable wraparound porch to take pleasure in the incredible flower gardens each morning where they can sip rich coffee and tea or as a shady retreat on the warm summer afternoons enjoying a fresh glass of lavender lemonade. The Mansion has a reputation as a romantic, peaceful, and passionate Bed and Breakfast. Its elegance and sophistication have made it popular for special events, anniversary, celebrations, weddings.

NOTES

NOTES

NOTES

NOTES

NOTES

NOTES

NOTES

NOTES

NOTES

NOTES

NOTES

NOTES